Ang

An

Angel

in the

Making

Frances Gomez

ISBN 0-9662631-0-3

10   9   8   7   6   5   4   3   2   1

CONTENTS

Chapter One

THE STORM OUTSIDE

I sit by the fireplace, searching its warmth for comfort. Outside, the storm grows stronger. I listen to a thousand winds buffeting the trees. My thoughts blow too. Memories just outside my thoughts lie waiting to be reviewed, memories of the events that effected my life forever. I look at the fire. The fireplace seems to serve as a stage where the events of the past year are played out. I remember the promise I made to Charlie, to write this story, and so I begin to fulfill this promise.

Chapter Two

THE CALL

The day started like every other. As a licensed clinical social worker, I was conducting a psychotherapy session with a client, when the phone rang. Surprised by the interruption, I hesitated to pick it up, letting my assistant answer it. The voice on the intercom said, "It's your daughter, and it's an emergency!" It was the dreaded phone call that every parent fears. I picked up the phone nervously. At the other end of the line, a tearful voice said, "Mom, it's Charlie. I'm in the hospital. The doctor says I have cancer." My heart stopped. I felt as if all my blood was drained from my body, but my mind thought, "Your daughter needs you. She's scared." I heard myself saying, "I'm on my way."

My client was already out the door, mentioning something about rescheduling.

As I drove to the hospital in Salt Lake City, my body felt cold and clammy. My heart pounded so hard that I could barely breathe. I had to pull over and cry. It was all I could do to pray for strength. A million thoughts raced through my mind. How can this be? She has never been ill, other than with a cold. I had been with her just three days earlier. I spoke with her on the phone yesterday and she was all right then. There had to be a mistake. Definitely, it was a mistake. After all, doctors do make mistakes.

Arriving at the hospital, I hurried to her room. I saw my youngest daughter, Ingrid, and her husband Christopher. They looked pale, scared, and deadly serious. Then I saw Charlie. I hugged her as we both cried. She explained that early that morning she had started hemorrhaging. Ingrid had rushed her to the hospital, where after examining her, the doctor gave her his verdict—cervical cancer. I mumbled something about doctors being wrong. I wiped the tears from her eyes and my eyes and tried to pull myself together. I said, "I'm going to see the doctor."

The hospital corridors felt incredibly cold. As I tried to locate the doctor in what seemed like a maze, I told myself he would dismiss this horrible fear that clutched my heart like a tight fist. Oh God, dear God, let this be a mistake. Please, not this!

Finally, I found the doctor. "I'm Charlie's mother, Mrs. Gomez," I said to him, trying to control the anguish and terror I felt. "Charlie says that you think she has cancer." It felt like an eternity until he answered, only to confirm the diagnosis. Numbness took over my body, as he went on to explain that a tumor the size of a tennis ball was growing on her uterus. His immediate concern was her hemorrhaging. If they couldn't stop the bleeding, she wouldn't make it through the night. My knees bent underneath my body; I felt like the life had been knocked out of me. Unable to speak, I screamed silently in my mind. Not her, God! She's a young woman, let her live. Let it be me. God, please. How can this be true?

Pulling me out of my thoughts, the doctor's

voice droned on. "This is a terminal illness. If we can stop the bleeding and she makes it through the night, we will undergo radiation. I have to go, but the resident doctor will follow my orders." Duty called. He was gone.

I leaned against the cold wall, unable to move. Wishing I could escape the moment, I sobbed uncontrollably. Completely oblivious of my surroundings, I cried and prayed for strength.

Two hours earlier, life had seemed so good. I had started a new challenging job, providing psychotherapy for sex offenders. I had been planning a vacation to San Diego. My three daughters had found direction in their lives. Each of us had learned to live with the sudden death of my husband, their father, ten years earlier.

A determination grew within me. My daughter Charlie needed me now more than she ever had. I had to be strong for her. I had to put my pain and fear on hold. A mother's love is one of the strongest forces in life, I reminded myself. A mother's love can do whatever has to be done when her children need her. Strength seemed to grow in my soul, unseen by those around me. This power seemed to electrify me. As I took charge of my grief, I felt and recognized the presence of God. I smiled as I muttered, "Thank you."

All through a night that seemed to have no end, I hovered by Charlie's bed. Every effort was being made to stop the bleeding. If they could stop it, maybe they would be able to control the tumor. The room gradually emptied as family members and friends left, allowing nurses and hospital staff to do their work. Every fifteen minutes, her blood pressure was taken to see if it was continuing to drop. Each drop in pressure brought her closer to death. I was stroking her head, wiping her hair back from her cold face when Charlie said, "Mom, I remember you used to say this prayer when I was little. The part that stuck in my memory was, 'If I should die before I wake, I pray the Lord my soul to take.'" We hugged and cried.

At 4:30 A.M. the bleeding was finally controlled. The immediate danger had decreased. A relief swept over us. I called Patricia, my oldest daughter, and Ingrid to inform them. As we wept, we thanked God that another day had been granted to us. Where do we go from here? "What now?" we wondered.

Chapter Three

FIRST STEP
THROUGH THE DOOR

I couldn't understand how Charlie could not have had any other pain or symptoms before the diagnosis. I remember her saying at times that she felt tired, but she attributed it to the stress of her demanding job as the coordinator of Even Start, a Salt Lake City School District family literacy program. However, it was not her job that caused her tired feelings.

Charlie's hospitalization had coincided with the graduation of the Even Start program. Parents and children were dumbfounded. Charlie wasn't there. They were even more surprised when at the end of the ceremony it was announced that Charlie was in the hospital.

Immediately, the entire class of about 50 families headed for the hospital.

It couldn't be true. The class had to see for themselves. Charlie's hospital room had a never-ending stream of visitors as family after family came to verify the awful news. No one could believe it was Charlie lying there. The Charlie they knew was energetic, kind, warm, intelligent, and full of life. Many became emotional, crying as they saw her looking so pale and sick against the white sheets of the hospital bed. Tears flowed freely. Even the most "macho" of men, her students' fathers, cried as they expressed their gratitude and condolences. Little gifts were given to her with prayers. Each person who came to visit had been deeply affected by her teachings and love.

The doctor decided surgery was out of the question. Removing a tumor that size would require cutting out part of her bladder and intestine. Radiation therapy seemed to be the best option. Little did we realize or know what lay ahead from such a simple phrase, "radiation therapy."

Radiation is something that can heal or kill.

In Charlie's procedure, radiation rods would be inserted into the vagina. Packing would be placed around the rods to prevent them from moving and burning healthy tissue. Radiation rays would then flow through the rods, to burn and shrink the tumor. The procedure seemed more like something used in the medieval ages than in the day of modern medicine. When the moment came, Charlie was anesthetized so that the rods could be inserted.

For three long agonizing days, Charlie lay on her back, unable to move; her abdominal area was bathed with radiation. Pale, cold, and nauseated, my daughter cried out to me in excruciating pain, begging, pleading with me, "Please, Momma, stop this pain. Please!" The treatment was brutally hard on body and mind.

Helplessly, I stood by her side, tortured, completely unable to do anything. I wished that I could trade places with her. I could feel my heart being ripped apart. How much pain could she endure? I remembered when Charlie was born and how happy I had felt when I held her in my arms for the first time. I believed then that I would always be able to protect her. Yet there wasn't a single thing I could do now to ease her pain. In that moment, worse than the thought of losing her, was watching her writhe and suffer in helplessness.

Three days later, which seemed like a lifetime, Charlie was discharged from the hospital. When we arrived home, she had to run to the bathroom. Then I heard her call me. "Mom, look at this!" I entered the bathroom and saw her standing with her arm extended. On her hand was a charcoal, barbecued chunk of meat. It was a piece of the tumor.

With the tumor gone, the doctor assured us that Charlie would go into remission. Radiation treatment was scheduled for two weeks later. I moved Charlie's belongings out of her apartment and put everything into storage. Then I brought her home to stay with me. For two weeks she had terrible bladder spasms, and tissue burns wherever the radiation rods had touched her. The thought of another radiation treatment was so terrifying to her that she had nightmares almost every night. I woke with her and tried to comfort her in whatever way I could. The fear of another treatment consumed her every waking and sleeping moment.

Soon the day came to be hospitalized again. Charlie refused to go. It took a great deal of persuasion from the doctor to convince her. He told her that if she didn't complete the treatment the tumor would return and she would die. He also told her that the tumor had disappeared, and with another treatment they could make sure that she would go into remission. Terrified, she finally agreed to be hospitalized for a repeat of the procedure she had endured just two weeks before.

I waited for four long, agonizing hours until the procedure was completed. The chief doctor met me in the hospital waiting room. He said there was no trace of the tumor, and that the radiation treatment would ensure she would go into remission. Elated, I ran to her room to hug her and give her the good news. She wasn't there. I waited and waited. Finally, they brought her in. Charlie didn't look good at all. She was restless and seemed to have a hard time coming out of the anesthesia. She was very cold, had difficulty breathing, and she appeared to be in horrible pain. Something was seriously wrong. The nurse stated, however, that Charlie was responding normally and only needed to rest. I told Charlie what the doctor had said, but she didn't seem to comprehend. The nurse gave her a painkiller—300cc of Demerol, and requested that I leave the room. Concerned that I had been exposed to too much radiation, the nurse gently pushed me towards the door. I sat outside in the hallway, feeling that something wasn't right. As tired as I was, I couldn't relax. I felt a strange fear. Pacing back and forth, I finally decided to go back in. My daughter was all alone in there.

Charlie was blue and seemed to be having convulsions. I called to her and put my hand on her chest. I couldn't feel her heart, so I ran out of the room calling for the nurse. When he saw me, he rolled his eyes and slowly walked into her room. As soon as he took a look at her, he rushed to her bedside and called, "Code blue!"

At that moment, I became hysterical. I ran out the door and down the hall, screaming "Hurry! Hurry! My daughter is dying! My daughter is dying!" Suddenly, I noticed nurses on each side of me. They grabbed me by the elbows and lifted me into the air, pulling me backward to stop me from running. Although my feet couldn't touch the ground, I tried to break away by pivoting on the tip of my tennis shoe. I struggled to stop them from controlling me but they succeeded. Together they managed to put me into a chair, where one of them sat on me and the other placed a wet towel on my neck. They spoke continuously, all the time trying to calm me down. I couldn't pay attention to what they were saying. I sat outside Charlie's room, watching as a resident tried to revive her. I waited there, sobbing in unbelievable terror for what seemed like forever.

Finally she responded. The intern said that she hadn't been deprived of oxygen long enough to sustain brain damage, and her initial responses were good. I ran to Charlie and hugged her while I cried silently. I didn't want to let go of her.

Charlie opened her eyes and smiled at me. She whispered, "Mom, Papá was here, standing by my bed just looking at me. He seemed so peaceful and calm. When he left, I wanted to go with him."

"Did you?" I asked, remembering the blissful feelings from my own near-death experience, when my mother had come to guide me. "What happened when your heart stopped?"

"I was in some kind of tunnel until someone pulled me out. It was so peaceful in there and so painful here. I'm tired . . ." she muttered, as she drifted off to sleep.

"Yes," I sighed, "it's peaceful there and painful here." I don't know how long I stood there holding her hand.

The resident doctor pulled me out of my thoughts by reminding me, "You need to leave the room. You have been exposed to radiation beyond the limit."

"What happened?" I asked him.

"It seems," he said matter-of-factly, "they had already given her a heavy dose of Demerol in the recovery room, but forgot to record it on the chart. Unaware of this, the nurse on the floor gave her an equal dose and it caused respiratory arrest."

"And that's it?" I asked in anger. "The chief

doctor tells me she is going to be okay. She made it through the treatment. The tumor is under control. Then you almost killed her with the painkiller? And that's it? That's it?" I walked toward the doctor with my fist clenched, wanting to discharge my feeling of helplessness on him, but the fear in his eyes stopped me. Instead a string of profanity I wasn't even aware I knew came pouring out of my mouth.

"Lady, I'm just a resident intern here, so don't be mad at me," was his response. I was infuriated by the knowledge that each person involved would have that same reply. I knew there was nothing I could do about it. Forcing a calm upon myself, I sat outside Charlie's door, praying that such a thing wouldn't happen again. I was determined to watch every move made by nurses and doctors until Charlie was safely out of the hospital.

A little while later, I looked up and saw Ingrid coming toward me. She rushed up and sat down next to me. The nurse had called her and asked her to come. "What happened?" she asked as she put her arm around my shoulder. "I was told to come and calm you down because you were acting crazy."

Sobbing again, I explained what had happened. While she stroked my hair and comforted me, with my head resting on her shoulder, I fell asleep for the first time in days.

Four days later, the ordeal was over. The doctor declared Charlie in remission. The whole nightmare had lasted six weeks. At times, it was hard for us to believe it had ever occurred.

For Patricia, who lived in California, it was even more unbelievable. Although we kept her informed on a daily basis, it was still hard for her to accept because she never saw Charlie ill and had not been present during any of the treatment. She had been whirled through the diagnosis and the trauma without actually experiencing the reality of any of it. We all felt as if a hurricane had come and gone before we could comprehend it, a phantom monsoon that left damage and destruction in its wake.

In August, two months after her initial diagnosis, Charlie went back to work as the coordinator of the Even Start program. Life seemingly returned to normal. At times, even Charlie wondered if it had really happened, but the physical limitations and scars from the treatments were a constant reminder that it had. Persistent bladder spasms and painkillers became part of her daily life. The scars from the burns inside her thighs were so sensitive that clothes would make her bleed. Hot flashes and insomnia became the norm. Yet, she felt it was worth it, since she was still alive. She had "beaten cancer."

Chapter Four

NEW LIFE

While I was lying in bed one evening, the phone rang, jarring me awake. At the other end of the line a voice said, "Mom, it's Ingrid. I want you to be the first to know, I'm pregnant!"

First I was speechless by the surprise. Chris and Ingrid had planned they would not have any children until Chris finished the dissertation for his Ph.D. in engineering, and that wouldn't be for two more years. But after the surprise came a burst of joy. A grandchild. Finally, a long awaited grandchild. Yeah! I jumped out of bed while getting dressed and called to tell Patricia and Charlie the good news. Then I took the teddy bear and baby blanket which I had bought in the hopes of one day becoming a grandmother, and drove over to Chris and Ingrid's house. I couldn't wait until morning to hug and congratulate them.

A grandmother—I'm going to be a grandmother. So many thoughts and feelings crowded my mind. My baby was having a baby! I could hardly believe it. I wondered if it would be a boy or a girl. Who would it look like? What would he or she grow up to be? And I prayed in gratitude, asking that my daughter wouldn't have any complications, and that her baby would be a happy and healthy being. I also prayed that this baby would always know how much he or she was cherished, regardless of the mistakes we would make in raising it. Only months earlier, we had gone through a horrible nightmare with Charlie's illness; now a wonderful dream had come true. "Such is life," I said aloud.

Chris and Ingrid were surprised that I would show up so late in the evening. They looked happy and this felt good.

A couple of months later, more good news. Charlie would finally be going to medical school in California. A lifelong dream had come true. She was ecstatic. When she was eighteen she had become a paramedic, and later, she worked in an emergency room. Charlie always hoped that someday she would become a doctor like both her maternal grandfather and uncle.

"See, Mom, I told you that if they thought I was a male, I would be accepted." I had to agree. It seemed that her decision to change her birth name to her father's name had been a good idea.

Thanksgiving was fast approaching. As a family, we had so much to be thankful for. Charlie continued in remission. The threat of cancer seemed so far away. Each month, Charlie had faithfully gone to her check-up. Every time, she was told that she was still in remission. She gradually regained her physical strength. Also, we were thankful for our little angel soon to be born.

Charlie planned to prepare our Thanksgiving dinner by herself. She wanted to make it very special, since she had so much to be thankful for. She thought that this might be our last Thanksgiving together for years, as it would be even harder for all of us to reunite with both Charlie and Patricia living in California.

We chose to make a lonely friend from

Colombia, South America, who was going through a divorce, our guest of honor, to share our food and friendship as an expression of gratitude for all of the blessings we had received.

Patricia and Charlie spent a lot of time planning together for the future. They laughed and reveled in each other's company while making plans to live together in California. The Thanksgiving holiday seemed to welcome both reminiscing about the past and envisioning the future.

Chris and Ingrid were doing well too. Ingrid was over her morning sickness. I spent some of my time planning little traditions for the baby. I wanted this child to know how important he or she was to us. I knew that feeling loved and protected was a necessary ingredient for becoming a well-adjusted child. Later, it would offer the skills to cope with the hardships of life as an adult. Ingrid thought I was extravagant because I had started yearly traditions before the baby had even been born. It was a wonderful and unforgettable Thanksgiving.

Then the Christmas holidays came. In preparation for medical school, Charlie quit her job and began the process of saying good-bye to her friends and co-workers. She spent time thanking all of the families she had worked with, for not only had she impacted their lives, but they had so greatly influenced hers as well. As she said more than once, "It looks like I am teaching them, but in reality they are my teachers."

Saying good-bye was very hard for Charlie because she loved the people she worked with and she always put her heart completely into her job. On the other hand, however, she had a dream to fulfill. Charlie had always wanted to treat the disadvantaged. She had seen how family economics influenced treatment. She thought the world was forgetting its duty to community services. Many times she said that we would only improve the conditions of this world through love and cooperation. Often Charlie expressed sadness, thinking of underprivileged kids who couldn't get medical help because it wasn't "feasible." She envisioned the clinic she might one day open for children. During the holiday, she talked about these things in the true Christmas spirit.

She also made plans for the next year's

Christmas party. She bought Victorian ornaments at the after-holiday sales, decorating the tree in anticipation of her return home the following year. We decided that Patricia would be in charge of the food next time; I would be in charge of decorating the house, and given that Ingrid would have to take care of the baby, she was off the hook.

It was the first week of February, 1994, and Charlie was packing to leave for medical school. In just days, she would be gone. She was excited and talking non-stop, except when she was interrupted by coughs.

"What did the doctor say about this cough?" I asked.

"Oh, I'm fine, Mom," she replied. "He said it's a cold but I am still in remission. Don't worry."

"I want you to get that cough checked out before you go," I told her.

She laughed. "Oh Mom, I just saw the doctor two weeks ago and I'm fine."

I picked up the phone and gave it to her. "Now!" I said.

Sticking her tongue out at me while smiling

and shaking her head, she called the doctor for an appointment. The doctor seemed annoyed and asked what a cough had to do with cancer. Suddenly she got serious, and I heard her insist, "I want you to check it out. I have also continued perspiring at night and I want to know for sure that I'm okay before I move to California next week." He reluctantly made an appointment for her on Valentines Day.

Chapter Five

Eye of the Storm

It was Valentine's Day. Charlie had asked Ingrid to accompany her to the doctor. To a degree, we all felt something wasn't right. I was extremely nervous; I went to work, trying to keep myself busy to control the anxiety. At work I continually looked at my watch, waiting for Charlie to call. Finally, the phone rang. I picked it up with my heart racing, fearful of what the news would be. But still, I never expected Charlie to burst out sobbing. She cried, "Mom, the cancer has metastasized to my lymph nodes, lungs, and there is a mass around the Cava, the vein leading to my heart. The doctor can't do anything. He basically said to go home and die. Mom, I'm going to die."

Feeling like my brain had exploded, I said,

"Oh God. They said you were going to be okay. How could they not know? This just can't be. Tell Ingrid to bring you home." Almost at the same time, I felt my breakfast coming up and barely had time to pull out the trash can from under my desk.

With my heart pounding so hard that my chest hurt, I ran to my car. My whole body was shaking uncontrollably; I wailed out loud as I drove home on the freeway. Looking in the rearview mirror, I saw all the cars prudently staying behind, slowly and in perfect order, almost as if in a procession of condolence. As if they knew and could understand my grief. It was a strange feeling. It was as if they were leaving the road free for me to express my pain.

This is not supposed to happen, I thought. Children aren't supposed to die first. "Oh God!" I cried, "Why don't you take me instead?" Not only did I want her to live so that she would be spared the horrible suffering that came with disease, but I wanted to be rescued from the feeling of helplessness of not being able to make it better for her, and her sisters.

Suddenly I pulled my car over to the side and

took a deep breath. I felt I was hyperventilating. I told myself that I needed to calm down or I wouldn't be of any help to Charlie. I tried to imagine her feelings of devastation and fear. She was going to die, and she feared death. I didn't fear death. I had a near-death experience as a young woman when I supposedly drowned, and was pronounced dead for twenty-two minutes. While the cars flew by, my mind was transported to my youth.

I was almost eighteen years old. It was a Saturday and I was going with my husband and some friends to a resort called Melgar, to swim and dance for the weekend. Melgar was about three hours away from Bogota, Colombia, where we lived. We had motorcycle fever in those days, and had been drinking. Suddenly, as we approached the bridge over the Sumapaz River, the road became too narrow for all of us and Carlos lost control. While Carlos and the motorcycle rolled wildly down a dirt road next to the bridge, I flew from the back seat straight into the river.

Because the bridge was as high as a three-story building, and since I was not wearing a helmet, the impact of the water stunned me severely. As the current carried me, I gasped for air for what felt like mere seconds. Then a tremendous peace and feeling of bliss inundated me.

I felt I was floating, then I saw snapshots of my life—almost at the speed of light. Not only did I see them, but I relived every moment. It was as if everything that had ever happened to me, I could see three-dimensionally. I could see myself moving and speaking. Along with happy times, I could see and feel the sad, fearful, or angry scenes in great detail. Almost eighteen years of my life were there. Instead of lasting a long time, this surreal sequence of moments and memories took only seconds.

I felt myself leaving my body through my temples as if a giant magnet was pulling me out, and I felt and heard a gentle snap in my chest. I was confused but free. As I floated above, I saw my body get taken by the current, and at the same time I noticed Carlos, suffering only a few scratches, searching the water for me. He then found me and, grabbing me by my long hair, pulled me out of the river. One of his friends, a medical student, started CPR. As I looked at my body, I thought, how could I be *there* while I am here? I reached my hands up to my chest, trying to touch myself. I realized I still had a body, but it was different; I was made of fluid light. I seemed to exist beyond our dimensions of time and space. I couldn't understand. I noticed something different about the body lying in the sand. I had never seen my body completely before, and on one hand it looked so beautiful, while on the other hand, it appeared as lifeless as a wet suit. In that moment, another one of Carlos' friends asked, "Is she dead?"

At once, I realized what had happened. But I can't be dead. I'm awake! I still have a body, another body or something, I thought. It felt weightless, like when I would scuba dive and do somersaults. Stripped of my physical body, my consciousness did not cease, in fact, it became keener. My senses had no limits. They seemed to pick up the thoughts of the people in some kind of telepathic transfer. I could hear my husband thinking, "She can't be dead. Please, God, don't let her die." And the friend doing the CPR was thinking, "Come on, woman, breathe. Come on, breathe." At that moment, the ambulance came and my physical body was taken to the town hospital.

My floating body was pulled back by a voice saying, "Come on, Frances, let's go!" I turned and saw my mother. In that instant, I felt like someone had tugged me by the collar. I started going down some kind of tunnel with several lanes, at tremendous speed. It was sort of like being sucked down or caught in the eye of a tornado. There was marvelous music and a rainbow of colors so vivid that I can't even begin to explain. None of it was painful or frightening, just peaceful and natural feeling.

All the time, the bliss was increasing. There were other people and animals going down the other lanes, but it wasn't important to know who they were. There was no feeling of loss, or sadness about leaving my husband and daughters. There was only an aura of serenity that kept increasing, and a knowledge that everything was connected somehow. I was going home to the world where I had once existed as a magnificent, spiritual being of light. I was only home for a short while, however.

What had transpired, later seemed obvious. I was born because I had chosen to come to this world as part of a plan. I had accepted a physical body for this life and agreed to face the challenges necessary for growth. At the time of this accident, though, my growth was not yet complete, and so my body and spirit reunited. I was not ready to go *home* . My spirit then returned to my body as it lay on a gurney outside the door of the hospital morgue.

Many times afterward, I yearned for that ethereal home. Instead, I was left behind when my husband Carlos, an engineer by profession, was killed in an industrial accident years later. Now my daughter would be leaving too.

Parked at the side of the road, a glimmer of peace returned to me as I remembered the bliss I felt during my near-death experience. It also brought hope, knowing Charlie too would travel this same journey home. Then I felt a stab of sadness and loss; once again, panic quickly replaced every other feeling. The memories of Charlie in the hospital, begging me to ease her excruciating pain, came rushing back to my mind. I tried to imagine what she must have felt when the doctor gave her the diagnosis. I worried that the news would upset Ingrid in such a way that it would effect her pregnancy. I had no idea of what to do or say to help. I lost track of time as I cried and prayed for help.

Shaky and nauseous, I finally made it home. Charlie and Ingrid weren't there yet. Desperate, I ran around the house howling like a wounded animal. Then I grabbed the broom and swept the living room rug with such force that I ruined it.

Exhausted, I called my friends for help. Fortunately, I had an extensive support system. They listened and attempted to calm me. I felt some relief. I needed to talk about it so it would sink in, but also, so that the fear would diminish. It's like when one has a nightmare and talks about it until it is no longer scary. Hearing my friends crying with me, echoing my pain, seemed to uplift me. I mostly appreciated their support; they would say, "I am here for you. Let me know what I can do for you." Knowing that was comforting. Although many of them offered to come over, I felt that in that moment I wanted to be alone with my daughters.

Finally, Charlie and Ingrid arrived. They were both teary and terrified. I hugged them and we cried. They sat on the couch while I sat across from them, watching them in silence. Charlie's face was pale and shiny like a white candle. Her body was limp. She was speechless with shock, numb. Ingrid couldn't stop talking and crying at the same time. She kept repeating, "It's a mistake. Those stupid doctors. They said you were in remission. They don't know what they are doing. We need a second opinion."

I was heartbroken, feeling a mixture of pain and fear beyond anything I had ever experienced. I watched as Charlie sat devastated. I could sense the fear and horror in her mind—all her dreams crashing, ending. I agonized for Ingrid because the anticipation of her baby was clouded by such pain.

Suddenly, watching them sit there side by side, I thought, Oh God, you are taking Charlie, but in your infinite wisdom and compassion, you are giving us another life. An immense peace came over me. I understood, or maybe was reminded—reminded that my daughters weren't mine. They existed as beautiful and powerful spirits before coming to this earth, and they had honored me with the assignment of bringing them into this world, to help them face challenges and grow as infinite beings. This insight brought serenity. We comforted each other during that long afternoon on Valentine's Day, a day dedicated to love. I knew the months ahead were not going to be easy, but I also knew without a doubt that our Creator and our angels would be with us to give us the strength to endure the difficult moments. I slowly murmured, "Thank you, God. I know this too shall pass."

Later, Chris came to take Ingrid home. He didn't know what to say either. I sat on the couch next to Charlie, in silence, just holding her hand. Occasionally she would whisper, "I can't understand how this could happen. It's like a nightmare." I had no answers for her or for myself.

The next morning, feeling like every bit of

energy had been sucked out of our bodies, we were left with only a nauseous feeling in the pits of our stomachs. Charlie, Ingrid, and I dragged ourselves to the hospital to get Charlie's medical records. The doctor hadn't explained anything and he wasn't available. Charlie seemed to need something tangible to believe what was happening. As she read the reports and saw the x-rays, sadness came over her. Finally she said, "I guess there is not much that can be done. I just don't understand how they didn't pick up on this, and I am getting angry about it. I also resent the insensitive way in which the doctor dropped this bomb on me. It feels as though I have been assaulted."

Her anger lasted several days, and finally she went to see the doctor to express her feelings. She felt betrayed not only by him, but also by medicine, which had been the love of her life. She accused him of being insensitive because he had been talking to his students about her, as if she was an object or medical guinea pig. He offered no explanation for what had happened, no apology for his behavior. This left her devastated. He did, however, insist on treating her, but she refused. Still she wanted to believe that maybe the doctor had started his mission with love, but along the way had lost his compassion and integrity. This saddened her.

Charlie shopped for another doctor and found one. Although there wasn't much that this doctor could do, his warm presence and kindness was comforting to her, and me. He offered chemotherapy as a last resort, but Charlie refused treatment. He respected her wish, but let her know that if she ever changed her mind, he was available. Instead, Charlie decided that this time she would try a nontraditional approach.

Chapter Six

MACROBIOTIC DIET

Charlie had picked up a magazine at the doctor's office and read an article about the macrobiotic approach to cancer. Basically, it is a way of life that incorporates a diet and philosophy to help bring about improved health. She thought people needed to know about this diet.

The article read: "Can macrobiotics cure cancer? The dominant view is that the disease is our enemy, and so we immediately cut it out and bombard it with radiation or chemicals. We try to eliminate it by destroying it, and in the process, destroy ourselves." The author of the article began with a summary of the American diet—pointing out that since the early part of the century, our diet has steadily degenerated. In the 1900's, Americans for the most part ate whole grains, fresh vegetables, and fruit. They consumed much smaller amounts of red meat, dairy products, artificial colors, and preservatives. This is not to say that they weren't eating meat, cheese, eggs, and other such foods, but that they were eating much less of these than we do today. The diet was centered around complex carbohydrates, particularly those derived from whole wheat, potatoes, barley, oats, and rice.

With arriving technology and the twentieth century came the more synthetic diet that we eat today. Most of our foods come out of a can or box. Moreover, vegetables are generally regarded as an accessory to the principle food, which is meat. The modern diet contains little, if any, whole grain products. The grains we eat have been refined and stripped of many vitamins and nutrients, as well as all the important hull or bran. We tend to eat many of our meals outside the home, and therefore, inevitably consume oily foods. So, over the past eighty years, our diet has changed dramatically, from one that was composed chiefly of grains and vegetables to one that is centered around animal products. Between 40 and 45% of our total dietary calories can be attributed to fat, most of it saturated animal fat.

In countries where a diet similar to the macrobiotic diet is eaten, there is an extremely low percentage of heart disease and cancer; this has led many scientists to believe that cancer and cardiovascular disease could be prevented by proper eating habits. In order to restore health, we must reestablish that state of balance.

After reading this article, Charlie remarked, "Wouldn't it be ironic, Mom, if after spending billions of dollars and using the greatest technology in the world to solve the problem of cancer, the answer was that simple? Have you heard about this diet before?"

"What a coincidence," I said. "A few months ago, a friend of mine mentioned that she was on a diet like this. At the time, she had even given me the name and phone number of her counselor." The nutritionist lived nearby, up on a hill near the state capitol, in an area called "The Avenues."

Charlie smiled and said, "Well, as you often say, nothing happens by accident."

On February 19, 1994, Charlie met with

Ursula, her macrobiotic specialist. Charlie found her to be intelligent and confident. She looked like she was in her early thirties and she spoke with a European accent. Ursula was very strict about Charlie following her instruction and diet. At the same time, Charlie felt her to be warm and caring.

Ursula listened to Charlie's description of the cancer; then she conducted a very unusual examination. First, she inspected Charlie's face thoroughly. Then she looked into her eyes, lifting her lids and asking Charlie to look up and down, right then left. Next, she examined her arms with painstaking thoroughness and asked her to remove her socks, so she could examine her feet as well. Again, she gave both feet careful inspection.

As Ursula looked at each area of Charlie's body, she would occasionally probe a spot on her arms, hands, or feet with her fingertips. The probing was done gently, but she must have been touching sensitive pressure points because the poking brought about an inordinate amount of pain. As she examined Charlie, she didn't say a word, seemingly lost in her own thoughts.

When the examination was over, Ursula said, "I wish you had come to me when you were first diagnosed, but I will try to help you. You will have to eat a very strict macrobiotic diet." She then told Charlie in great detail which foods she should and should not eat. She explained that her standard macrobiotic diet normally includes fish, fruit, whole grains, and vegetables, especially sea vegetables like seaweed. Because Charlie's condition was so severe, though, she would be expected to follow a strict diet specifically designed for her.

The diet consisted primarily of miso soup, prepared with hacho-miso. I was told that miso was a fermented soybean rich in enzymes and bacteria, both helpful for digestion. In addition to this, she would also eat brown rice and vegetables. We both left Ursula's house feeling very confused. We drove in silence for a while, and then Charlie turned to me and asked, "Should I do this diet, Mom? Is this enough or should I go with the chemo?"

I pulled the car over and held her icy hands. Looking into her eyes, I said, "This is a decision I can't help you with, Charlie. It is your life and you are the only one who can make that choice. But whatever it is, I will support you. I will do anything for you."

She hugged me and cried. "I wish I had absolute confidence in my judgment, but I don't. I don't know what to do. What do you do when you feel like this, Mom?"

"Well, I turn to God for help, and I'm thankful that I'm not alone."

Nothing more was said. I could feel her fears and her struggles. Later that night, somewhat calmer, she said, "The doctor told me I still have some time to decide whether I want the chemo. So, I don't have anything to lose if I try this diet. Could we start it tomorrow?" I nodded affirmatively.

The next morning I went to the natural food store and stood in the entrance, not knowing where to start. I couldn't help laughing at how I had spent four years of my life learning to cook gourmet, and now I had a list of ingredients that were a total mystery to me. The first item read: "dicon."

I didn't have a clue whether it was an animal, vegetable, or mineral. The clerk at the store smiled as he showed me around. It turned out that dicon is an overgrown, albino, carrot-like vegetable.

I signed up for a cooking class that same day. Unfortunately, it didn't start for two weeks, so I decided to do my best until then. After all, I thought, anyone could cook some rice and vegetables.

That evening we sat at the table with miso soup, boiled salmon, steamed vegetables, and brown rice. It didn't look bad, although the thought of having this for breakfast, lunch, and dinner, was quite unappealing. We found the miso soup to be salty and distasteful. The seaweed was unpleasant and the rice was hard. The salmon was surely the most appetizing dish of the entire dinner.

Charlie had a hard time eating vegetables. She never liked them. Even as a baby, she would spit them out or throw up as I fed her. At dinner, though, she was willing to make an effort. We talked about the diet and we decided that maybe we just needed to get accustomed to it. At the end of the meal, our jaws hurt from chewing the crunchy brown rice. The following week, when

Charlie went to visit Ursula, we learned that the rice should have been cooked in a pressure cooker and that we had been eating raw rice the whole time. We got a pressure cooker.

One morning I got up at 5:00 A.M. to prepare Charlie's food before I went to work. While I was cooking, the pressure cooker blew a valve. Alarmed, Charlie ran into the kitchen yelling , "Mom, are you okay?" As I mumbled in frustration, we both looked up at the seaweed and other greens hanging from the ceiling and then looked at each other and burst out laughing. The laughter did our hearts good.

Eating was very difficult for Charlie, not only because of the types of food, but because, as is the case with most cancer patients, her ability to taste was changing. A dietitian once explained it as "eating a pear that is not ripe." Food tastes bitter and makes the tongue and lips stick to the teeth. The appetite lessens, but the need for food becomes greater. Cancer tumors can consume 1200 to 1500 calories a day over and above the body's normal requirements. Therefore, the need to eat increases, but the ability to eat decreases.

This is why a high percentage of cancer patients die of malnutrition.

Yet, regardless of how hard it was, Charlie was willing to give it a try. Day by day, I noticed that she ate less and less, becoming weaker and weaker. As for me, despite the stress of her illness and the pressure of my intense job, my energy level increased. What was surprising to me, more than the energy boost, which I attributed at the time to functioning on adrenaline, was that even on sleepless nights, my mind was so clear. I could tell there was a big difference within me. Finally, though, I too discontinued the diet, because Charlie's sense of smell was heightened. Just the smell of food would make her sick.

I remember expressing to Charlie how the diet had given me energy. She sadly remarked that maybe it was just too late for her. She regretted not having the chance to witness the diet's true potential. Charlie wished she had seen Ursula when she was first diagnosed. She also hoped that people would change their eating habits to incorporate a diet and philosophy that would help bring about improved health in their lives.

Chapter Seven

FORGET ME NOT

As the days went by, we vacillated from despair to denial, then back to despair, and in the middle of all this we still had to "chop wood and carry water." It was easy to have hope and pretend this wasn't happening to us. What was more difficult was believing that Charlie was dying, because she looked healthy. Except for becoming easily tired and profusely perspiring at night, there weren't any signs that she was ill. Even the cough had disappeared. She spent some of her time making crafts for friends and family. She even set up a couple of workshops for the Even Start participants.

One day Ingrid stopped by. While visiting with Charlie, she broke down crying and said,

"Why is this happening? Why you? You haven't even had a cavity in your whole life."

Charlie hugged and comforted her but started crying too. Ingrid tried to repair the damage, saying, "Well, you will be with Papá. He is alone while we are all here. You will be with him and he won't be lonely anymore."

Charlie stopped and looked at Ingrid intently. "Yeah, you are right. You are right, Ingrid," she emphasized.

"Grandmother is there too."

"Well . . ." Charlie said, raising her eyebrow, "so is Elvis, but I didn't know him either." They both laughed.

"You get the picture," Ingrid continued. "When that elevator opens, whether you go up or down, there will be enough of our relatives to keep you company." They burst out laughing again while Charlie gently punched Ingrid on the arm.

Charlie was reminded of her experience after the radiation therapy, when she saw her father standing by her bed. She recalled for us how peaceful he seemed. "Do you think he will come to help me when I die?" she asked. I told her I was sure he would. He loved his daughters so much.

Later that night when Ingrid had gone, Charlie sat by the window, lost in her thoughts. She turned around with tears in her eyes and extended her arms to me just like when she was a baby and wanted me to take her out of the crib. I held her and she cried softly. "I am so afraid, Mom," she whispered.

After a while I asked, "What are you afraid of, Charlie?"

"I am afraid of this illness that has begun to shut me down and will continue until I cease to function and die. The process itself is scary because it's so painful and uncomfortable. But when it's complete, I don't know what is going to happen to me. The unknown is petrifying. Am I going to disappear? All my life I thought I believed in God, but now is the moment of truth and I'm frightened. If there is life after death, will I make it or will I just fade away into nothing?"

"I think you know the answers to those questions. Honor that knowing. Did you just fade away when they overdosed you?" I asked.

"I don't know what to think. I'm scared and confused. One of my biggest fears is that you and my sisters will forget me."

"Oh Charlie, how could you ever think that we would forget you? You will never die because you will always be with us in our hearts and minds," I said while hugging her even closer.

She looked up at me and asked, "Aren't you afraid, Mom?"

"Yes," I said crying. "I have my fears. I'm afraid I won't have the strength to live without you. I'm also afraid and sad to think that one day I will come home and you will be gone, and I won't be here when it happens."

She looked at me seriously and said, "No, Mom, please don't do that to yourself. You have always been there for me when I needed you. When I used to work with the terminally ill, I would spend days and nights with a person that was dying. In the one moment I would leave, even to go to the bathroom, they would die. I think it's because they didn't need me to be there. Sometimes I felt guilty, even rejected when it would happen, but now I'm starting to understand. I promise you, Mom, the day I die, you will be with me."

We hugged and were silent for a moment, until Charlie asked for some water. Then she said, "Mom, don't you think it's amazing that with death being something no one escapes, we are not prepared to die? Is it because it's so scary?"

"Yes, I think so. We are so limited and afraid in this world that we avoid thinking about death. It is one of our greatest fears. Yet if properly confronted, fear and pain can be our best teachers. Just remember that the whole purpose of this life is growth. Don't let fear paralyze you. Death is just the process we must complete to go back home. It's the natural cycle: life, death, and rebirth. If we knew how wonderful it was to return home, we wouldn't want to stay here."

Making a funny face, Charlie said, "The problem is that *this* is all I know, and I kind of like it." We laughed. "Have you ever wished you could leave?"

"Yes, but I know how important it is to complete my time and fulfill my purpose in this world, and I will do just that. That doesn't mean

I don't yearn to return home. This is hard to explain, Charlie, because when I say this, people think I may be contemplating suicide. Yet, that is something I would never consider. It's more like being homesick all the time, waiting, always waiting. Or you could compare it to graduate school. You know it's necessary, but you can't wait for it to be over."

Charlie smiled. "Maybe I just need to remember what it felt like when I held Papá's hand and wanted to go with him from the hospital." Then, as though sharing a secret, she added, "You know, I think my papá is an angel now."

"I wouldn't be surprised, Charlie. When he died, he was trying to save other people. You know that on the day of the accident, while your papá was in the office at the company where he had worked, the women on the assembly line started screaming that ammonia was coming out of a tank. He ran to the tank, saying he would shut it off; he knew the danger. Ammonia is lethal. Unfortunately, the valve had blown off and he inhaled the ammonia, dying instantly. He could have chosen to run out of there like everybody else, but he really cared about people."

"Yeah, you are right, Mom."

Chapter Eight

FAMILIAR TERRITORY

One night I could hear Charlie tossing and turning more than usual so I went to her bed. Her pillow was soaked from perspiration. I took a new pillow and put a pillowcase on it, then I wrapped a towel around it. While I dried and caressed her head, I asked if she was in pain. She said, "No, I'm just sad," and she asked for water.

I held her hand and kissed it. "Charlie, what's your biggest sadness when you think about dying?"

"Leaving you and my sisters without knowing if I will ever see you again—not knowing the baby or seeing her grow . . ." she sobbed sadly. I held her and kissed her in silence. Then, thinking she had fallen asleep, I laid her down. I was quietly tiptoeing to the door when her voice called me back. "Mom, what is it like, when you die I mean? Does it hurt? What does it feel like? Tell me about your near-death experience. Why don't you really ever talk about it?"

"I rarely discuss it because it's very difficult to explain," I told her. "Language eludes the things that we have experienced through our senses. My journey is something which lies beyond the conscious awareness of most people. In addition, many people who have had near-death experiences have been told that they may have been caused by some sort of brain damage, or that they were hallucinating. That's the only way that some doctors can explain a phenomenon they are unable to understand."

"Well, if brain damage provided you with the incredible coping skill you have, I wouldn't mind having brain damage myself. You have had to deal with more pain than most people I know. I don't understand how you do it, but I want to hear about your near-death experience," Charlie pleaded.

I smiled and continued. "When it first happened, I experienced some ridicule from people who just didn't understand. Actually, I didn't understand either. No one talked about such a thing as a near-death experience. It was confusing for me. I thought maybe I had lost my mind. In addition, the experience seemed to develop my intuition and precognitive powers, and it was scary to me and those around me. It made life harder to cope with. It wasn't until I read Dr. Raymond Moody's book, *Life After Life*, in 1982, and attended a gathering of hundreds of people with similar experiences, that I felt validated. Knowing that many other people had taken the same journey gave me peace of mind. It was like all of a sudden, I was centered. I no longer doubted my experience, or feared ridicule. I could still, however, understand other people's doubts about it. If I hadn't lived the experience, I would think it was crazy myself."

Excited, Charlie sat up on her bed. "I know what you mean. I also thought it was a dream when they overdosed me at the hospital, and sometimes I still do. I go back and forth."

"I know, Charlie."

"Tell me more. Did it hurt to die, Mom? I'm afraid of the pain."

"No. There was a very short moment of feeling anxious about not being able to breathe, but there was no pain; it didn't hurt at all. You have been through much more pain with the radiation. Besides, the one second I was not able to breathe was insignificant compared to the bliss I experienced."

"Mom, you'll help me when the moment comes for me to die and I can't breathe and get scared, won't you?"

"Yes. I promise," I assured her.

"Tell me more," Charlie requested.

"It started with a peaceful feeling of incredible bliss that kept increasing and an awareness that I had entered another kind of existence. Once I left the tunnel that takes us out of this dimension, I felt I was floating in space. I looked over my right shoulder and saw planets, and slowly turning my head over my left shoulder, I saw a galaxy in the distance. This galaxy seemed connected to a world by what looked like a huge strand of DNA. The world was part of a cluster of three worlds joined by tunnels. As I was floating, it was as though I was learning by osmosis. I was knowledge. I had an understanding about time before I came to this world, as well as during and after leaving this world. I was part of everything and everything was part of me. Thought and motion became one.

"Then I clearly saw the worlds. On the first world, I seemed to shed another body. It looked like a silhouette of the original physical body I had left in *this* world; it seemed to be made of energy. This body is what we call the dark side, or ego. In that moment, my mother gently pushed me toward a tunnel to my left. She said, 'Go and learn, Frances.' She went toward a tunnel on the right. I could see a bright, fluorescent looking light coming out of that tunnel. I knew that that was where the angels were. Suddenly, some kind of vacuum pulled me into the tunnel on my left; this tunnel radiated golden light, and was connected to a glass-looking world. Once I was inside this spherical world, I floated to the right and shed another body. This body was also a silhouette of my original body, but it sparkled. It was the part of me that thinks. "Looking to my left, across from where I was, I noticed a sort of room. Although there wasn't any wall separating us, I knew there was an invisible divider.

I saw people in there, and my being understood that they had committed suicide. It was sort of a waiting room; it was cold. They were not able to shed their other bodies, and their liquid light bodies seemed to be trapped inside what seemed like mesh bodies. The light could flow beneath the mesh, but they could not release it. I could feel the sadness of these people. They seemed to have to wait until the time that they had agreed to spend on earth was completed. This seemed to be very important. Apparently, when we agreed to come to *this* world, we committed to a period of time, and if we alter this, we wait in that room until the time expires. The people there get to see what happens on earth, but are unable to influence or change anything. As long as we have a physical body, we can continue to make changes.

"There was a particular man in the room who had committed suicide by shooting himself. He could see his family being abused, but he couldn't do anything about it because of the choice he had made. The only other way people could move on from that room seemed to be, if they were released by their loved ones."

"What do you mean? Released how?" Charlie asked.

"When someone commits suicide, their loved ones agonize over it. When the family and friends realize that it wasn't their fault, they begin to heal. When they let go of the pain, shame, and guilt that stagnates their growth, and understand that it was the person's choice, the deceased can move on. I was overwhelmed by the beautiful truth that God always leaves an opening. God is truly a God of love."

"After learning all of this, I was sucked into another tunnel of golden light. This tunnel led to the third world. This was the world that was connected to the galaxy by what looked to me like a giant strand of DNA. In this world, all of my deceased family and friends, even people I didn't know, received me. This entire shedding process, from the first tunnel to the third world, usually happens very quickly—in a blur. I have been told, however, that it had been slowed down during my experience so that I could learn and grow from it."

"Did you see your mother and other relatives,

like when they were alive, Mom?" Charlie wondered.

"I saw them two-fold—in one way, as beings of light as they are now, and in another way, so that I could recognize them, as I had known them either in person or through pictures."

"You mean you could actually see? I don't understand how you could see. Your eyes stayed with your original body, didn't they?"

"It's hard to explain, Charlie, but we have more senses than we are aware of. Think of this, for example. Your eyes look at things that are outside your body, but when you are thinking or visualizing something, do your eyes turn and look inside your brain?"

Charlie laughed. "No."

"Well, if you pay attention you will notice that you see your thoughts with internal eyes. You may even close your eyes to concentrate. Have you noticed that? Well, it's something like that."

Still laughing, Charlie said, "I'll have to think about that one, Mom. Anyway, were your relatives happy to see you?"

"Yes, incredibly happy. Although it was a welcome and a farewell, the feelings of bliss just kept increasing the whole time. It was euphoric."

"If everything was so wonderful and perfect, why did they stop welcoming you and begin wishing you farewell?"

"Because from there, once my shedding was finally complete, all that was left of me was my pure being of liquid light. Then I shot off at tremendous speed, like a shooting star, to the world of brightness and light, to the land of my soul. I was home."

"Wow!" Charlie marveled. Then she remained silent for a while as if lost in her thoughts. Finally she whispered, "Mom, can you change this towel? It's wet. Then I want to hear more."

As I changed the towel, I continued. "This world was bright, full of light. That's where I met my Creator. It was a glorious moment. I was overwhelmed with intense feelings of joy, love, and peace. I can't think of any comparison that would describe it so you will understand. The feelings evoked from the most beautiful sunsets, music, poems, and art, combined with the glory of childbirth and everything else that is touching to you, would not even hold a candle to the feelings of absolute peace and bliss that I experienced. The words to explain my emotions in the presence of our Creator have yet to be invented. I felt mutual and immediate recognition."

"Although I don't recall the specifics of God's appearance, I do remember an aura of intense white light. It was like millions of diamonds radiating not only light, but love. I don't think what I saw was necessarily meant to be remembered. What felt of greater importance was the power of love that emanated from God. The power was the magnificence of perfect love."

"Perfect love?" Charlie repeated curiously.

"Yes. That is probably the most difficult thing to explain, because as humans our understanding of love is limited, and very conditional. Most of us, to some degree, love others conditionally. They have to look and act like us, or do what we want them to do; then we will be accepting. Perfect love is the feeling of being touched in the core of your soul by complete love and acceptance to the point of elation."

"Regardless of who I thought I was in this world, in that moment I knew who I was—a glorious, magnificent being of light. I remembered that I had always been a part of God. I knew I was in this world as part of the plan. In the presence of my Creator, I knew I was accepted unconditionally, and all that was required of me was to do the best I could to master this physical body, and complete my part of the plan. I knew with all of my being that there really was a God, whom I understood and loved."

Charlie asked, "What's this plan? I don't understand."

"It's like this, Charlie. Before we came to this world, we existed as magnificent, evolved beings of light. We lived in a vast universe with no restrictions. Then one day at an assembly, we were informed that there was a plan to raise a world into our dimension. Our love was all that was needed. With our love, we would make that world vibrate beyond its dimension, into ours, so that it could enter a higher order. Volunteers were requested."

"The condition was, we would have to take a

physical body. This was new to us. It was explained that while there were some pleasures, with these bodies, there were also other feelings, such as pain and fear, which were unknown to us in the spirit world. We would have to master these new feelings in order to love as our spirits do. We would be allowed to choose the birth parents and siblings that we would have in this world. We would also choose the challenges and lessons that would help us grow."

This world would be very confining and restrictive compared to the expansiveness of the eternal place that we knew. At birth our memories would start to fade until we had complete amnesia. We wouldn't remember who we were, but we wouldn't be alone. We would be born with a spark of God's light within us, to guide us in this world; that light would contain our soul's history. All we had to do was access this light and simply trust it. If we did this, even when we couldn't remember who we were, we could find comfort, strength, and balance when we needed it. By maintaining contact with our source, we would also strengthen our lights. The strength of our collective light, or love, would raise the vibration of the world; at the end of time, or sooner if we were successful, the world would be lifted into our spiritual dimension. Also, when we completed our time here, our lights would be strong enough to take us back home. Because, as eternal beings we possessed the freedom of choice, in the earthly world we *could* choose to ignore our source and not participate in the plan, but we were reminded that we were accountable for our choices."

"Some beings of light decided that they wanted to come on the great adventure, others preferred to assist us as angels. Some even agreed to continue helping as angels, once they made it home."

Charlie lied there in thought, soaking it all in. "Did God ask you anything?" she wondered.

"Yes. The question was, 'How much have you loved?' See, that's the whole purpose of why we are here. Despite the restrictions of our bodies, we agreed to love and support each other to accomplish our plan. It's very hard though. As humans, not only do we have to serve as the distinction between spirit and flesh, but we have to live in a restricted world, and grow in these circumstances. As the magnificent beings that we are, we can do it, even if it's hard."

"Gosh, Mom, but we live in such a competitive world."

"Yes, Charlie, but *we* have made it that way. We have done just the opposite of what we had agreed to do; we are constantly consumed by our fears, and that's what limits our growth." Charlie looked at me as if she didn't understand. I continued. "Tell me, do you think we are living from our light source when we are competing with others? In reality, the only person we have to compete with is ourselves. That's who we are accountable for. If people just concentrated on improving themselves, this whole world would be lifted in a heartbeat."

"I have always thought the world would be better if we cooperated," Charlie muttered.

"If you think about it, Charlie, we should be happy with other people's achievements, and even celebrate their success; after all, it's a blessing for everyone. So often we forget we are on the same team."

"What will happen if we fail to accomplish the plan?"

"The world will die."

"That's already happening, Mom."

"I know. We are failing as individuals and as nations. The worst part is that when we remember who we are, it will be hell. We'll have horrible regrets. You see, hell is not Dante's inferno, it's what we experience when we return home and see how poorly we lived our lives, and how we failed to accomplish our plan here."

"What happens if we don't make the light strong so it can take us home?"

"If we shoot off with a weak light, we fall into space and become dust. You know, like the dust that follows a meteor and later becomes a planet."

"That's interesting," Charlie said as she rearranged her pillow. Then she added, "Our bodies are made up of the same minerals as the earth. How do we make the light stronger?"

"With love. Owning our uniqueness, maintaining an open and loving heart. Remembering who and what we are. Love is what makes us magnificent beings. We are made of love because we are made of light, and love is light. When we give in to our dark side, we give our dark side a jolt. We give it a boost, and that diminishes our light."

"You mean like giving in to anger, bitterness, fear, or other negative feelings?"

"Yes. Although it's natural that, as we master our humanness, we are going to access these feelings, the goal is to learn how to strengthen our lights in such a way that we don't encounter them. Can you tell when you are around people and their light is stronger than their dark side, or vice-versa? Sometimes I work with criminals, and when I look into their eyes I see the darkness. There is hardly any light there. If the darkness is strong enough, you don't even have to look, you can feel it."

"But Mom, some people are victimized."

"True, because those that agreed to love them chose not to fulfill their promise. However, that doesn't mean that anyone has to stay in an abusive situation. It's fear that keeps people as victims. It limits our spirits. When anger is added to the fear, then it's easy for someone to become a victimizer as well. So you see it's dangerous to remain in our negative feelings. It's a far cry from what we agreed to do in this world, don't you think, Charlie?"

She was silent for a while, then she asked, "What about children? They are helpless."

"Yes, and that is why they need to be protected, and guided by all those who agreed to support them. One of our worst regrets will be our failure to help children. Once children grow up, though, they too acquire the responsibility to access their light. As they mature, they will become accountable for their agreement, and for owning their power."

"That's not fair," Charlie said passionately.

"Charlie, every person is responsible for their life. Every one of us made a commitment before we came here. Blaming others for our failure to meet our agreement is not going to cut it. There are lots of people who have been abused, live in horrendous conditions, and, although it's harder for them, flourish like flowers in rocky soil. It never ceases to amaze me that, regardless, they connect with their source."

"We have to make sure we are available to help. Especially children, and adults in abusive situations. That's why we were allowed to choose a support system before we came to this world. As part of someone's support system, we have a tremendous responsibility to help them. Remember, though, that we can only help if someone wants to be helped. It has to be their choice. Ultimately, though, everyone is responsible for their own life."

"What about Children that were killed and never grew up?" Charlie wondered.

"Oh, I wouldn't worry about them. They are angels. I am sorry for the perpetrators, however. Can you imagine what these people feel when they realize who they were and how low they fell?"

"I don't think I want to. Tell me more about the world of light," Charlie said as she sipped some water.

"I remember a feeling of brightness. The light was as white as snow, yet, it was a light that didn't burn or hurt my eyes. I remember wonderful, serene people doing things like weaving, for example. I don't know what was being woven; they looked like blankets, but transparent, as if they were filled with diamonds or sparkling beads. They were alive and filled with love.

These shiny blankets seemed to cover the entrance to a room. This room looked like a computer room, but it was a door to another existence. We continually progressed to other dimensions. I don't recall exactly how it worked, but I know it was of great importance. There were beautiful sounds, which I can only describe as music, flowing over me, or becoming a part of me. I specifically remember a pond of water, and putting my hand in, taking up water in it and looking at what seemed like little balls of mercury. They weren't sticking to my hand or melting into it, but rolling over it. This little dance of the water was very enjoyable. Drinking it was so soothing, sweet, and wonderful. There I was, having left my body here, but still having the perception of a body, seeing with a different set of eyes, and using my hand to cup magical water. I can even now close my eyes, concentrate on my hand, and bring back those feelings of bliss."

"There were also flowers and trees. They were alive. The flowers were so bright; they had colors I had never seen before. The blue ones seemed to be polarized light. Yellows felt as if the sun was inside them. Their brightness was as intense as looking at the sun in this world, except that there, it didn't hurt my eyes. Just like us, their spirits were incredibly beautiful. They were made of light. Every being seemed to radiate music, and the music expressed gratitude to our Creator."

"Mom, how come sometimes I feel like I'm here alone?"

"That happens when we are disconnected from our source. You are afraid of dying, so you have severed the connection to home. This is how fear can limit us. But, we are not here alone, Charlie. All we have to do is maintain the connection. We do this through prayer or meditation—whatever you want to call it. We also have angels to guide us. All we have to do is ask and listen. That , too, is a choice; we are continually making choices. For instance, right now I choose to be here with you, and I consider it an honor. I am glad I can be here for you. Your illness is a growth experience for me and the people who know you."

"Will God accept us, regardless of the choices we make?"

"Yes, God will love and accept us all. *We* are the ones that will have a hard time when we see who we are, and how poorly we lived up to our potential here. God only requires that we do the best we can."

"Why do some people have these near-death experiences?" Charlie queried.

"Well, some of us need the reinforcement. I know that it helped me during a difficult time in my life. There was a time when I didn't believe in God. In my childhood, I was taught to love and fear God. I felt like a feather in the wind, blown by this powerful and invisible being. So at first I chose to hate God, and later I chose not to believe there was a God. The price was loneliness. But after returning home from my near-death experience, my relationship with God transformed. I knew I had been in God's presence. I felt love, peace, and understanding in a way that was beyond words."

"You know, Charlie, these experiences have occurred for hundreds of years. I think the reasons they are being acknowledged now are to prepare people to understand death, and live in a new era. We are running out of time, and we haven't done a great job. Actually, only when death is no longer feared will humanity be able to leap into a different realm of consciousness."

"How do you think your near-death experience effected your life, Mom. Has it changed your perspective on things?"

"I have a greater understanding of life and its purpose. I know what my priorities are in this life. Because of this, I have an inner strength that shapes every day decisions. Despite all the confusion, after I drowned there was a change deep within me. I no longer was fearful of living, or taking risks. You see, the more fearful we are, the less strength we have. If we could just see ourselves as we really are, we would more fully understand that we have nothing to fear. We could use our full capacity to love. We would accomplish so much."

"Once a person has an experience like mine, death can no longer be feared. With no fear of death, all other fears are less intense. Therefore, we are able to use our intuition, take risks, be honest with ourselves, and deal with disaster with more equanimity. Feelings are expressed openly."

Charlie seemed to be deep in thought. After several minutes of silence, she asked, "During your experience, did you see anyone being born?"

"When I was traveling through the worlds and shedding bodies, there were beings of light that were heading in the other direction. They were picking up the bodies that other people had left behind. Then they would enter the tunnel that led to mortal life."

"Did they pick up your shed bodies?"

"No, I did. I needed them to return to this world."

Excited, Charlie sat up on her bed and, while sipping water, asked, "Did these beings come from the world of light?"

"No, they seemed to be coming up from the galaxy through the giant DNA strand that I mentioned earlier."

"That's interesting. Would that account for deja vu or the theory of reincarnation? If one of these bodies that they picked up was a "thinking self," a shedding of the intellect, then it would make sense that it kept memories of previous lives, don't you think?"

"I don't know, Charlie, but it's a thought."

"Why did you come back, Mom?"

"My time wasn't up yet. I have things to do here. My mother said to 'Go and learn,' so I guess my near-death experience served as a lesson."

"Were you upset when you came back?"

"When I returned to my body I had intense pain. It felt like every one of my nerves had to be reconnected. I have often wondered if this is how a newborn feels. I slept for over a week. Then I experienced a period of terrible guilt, because I hadn't missed my family during the journey."

"When you returned, how did the doctor discover that you were alive?"

"He didn't. He pronounced me dead. I was covered with a sheet and left outside what the town hospital considered a morgue, while the orderly went to find the key to the door. One of your papá's friends saw me move and let out a scream. Later he would make us laugh, telling how the hair stood up on his head; he thought I was a ghost. Your papá said that it was the longest twenty-two minutes of his life."

"What did Papá think about your experience?" she asked, yawning.

"He truly believed that I had been to the "other side." He said it was the only explanation for the things I kept talking about. There were other things that I partially remembered, but your papá refused to talk about them. He thought there was a reason why it had happened to *me*. He felt there were some things he should not know. Sometimes, however, he was curious and would ask questions."

Then, rubbing my neck, I asked, "Charlie, how much of my experience do you recognize or remember from when they overdosed you at the hospital?" Not receiving an answer, I glanced down at my daughter. She was sound asleep, looking very peaceful.

Chapter Nine

AN ANGEL

It was 5:20 A.M. when Christopher called us from the hospital. Ingrid was in labor. We nervously got dressed and drove over there. We sat in a huge room. Ingrid was hooked up to so many machines. It was amazing to watch the baby's little heart beating on the monitor. The monitor also gauged the intensity of Ingrid's contractions. When the pain began getting stronger, she asked for an epidural. I sat and watched, sensing an irony. Ingrid's agony in labor was reminiscent of the pain Charlie had been dealing with, but the intrinsic difference was worlds apart. For Ingrid, the increasing pain signaled imminent life; for Charlie, it foreshadowed impending death.

The doctor arrived and administered the

painkiller to calm things down. Eventually, Ingrid appeared to be hosting a picnic. I couldn't help but compare her labor to mine when she was born. A world of difference. Technology and medicine had progressed in assisting childbirth.

From Charlie's appearance, you couldn't tell she was ill, except that she had no energy. She was unable to even keep her eyes open. While waiting, she became so weak; I had to take her home to rest, and then return to the hospital. I was torn. On one hand, I wanted to be with Ingrid, and enjoy the birth of my first grandchild. On the other hand, I was terrified to leave Charlie. She looked so weak that I feared she would die while I was at the hospital. Charlie made it easy for me. She said she needed to sleep and would feel better if I was with Ingrid. I felt sad that Charlie couldn't be there, yet she called the hospital several times, worried the labor was taking too long. I also became concerned about this as the day went on. The nurses became more and more intense. They were getting very serious and worried. Finally, the doctor entered and decided to give Ingrid medicine to help her increase the contractions. Around 3:00 P.M., the doctor came back in and the room transformed into a surgical unit. She was going to give birth.

What an experience it is to see another person give birth, especially when that person is your own child. While the nurse held Ingrid on one side, and with Christopher on the other to help her push, I stood in front to watch the being born. Finally, her little beautiful face peeped through. The doctor used a tiny plunger to pull her out. Slowly, then, her small body emerged. An unbelievable feeling of relief and awe rushed over me. I watched while the spirit of my new grand baby welcomed the world.

I looked at Ingrid and Chris as they touched and held their baby in amazement. The sun was shining through the window upon them. The little bundle of mystery and enchantment, magic and fantasy, was named Morgan.

While they cleaned and dressed her, I called Charlie in tears and told her it was a girl. Charlie called Patricia and the news spread. The much-awaited baby was fine, and the mother too. I rushed home to bring Charlie to meet the baby. We returned just in time for the first photograph. The feeling of joy that permeated our lives was just incredible.

I watched Charlie holding the baby, smiling as these spirits met and merged for the first time, but grieving with the knowledge that one of them would too soon continue on. Charlie's happiness of living to see her sister's baby seemed to overshadow this thought. It even eclipsed the torment she expressed of not being able to watch her grow.

When we left the hospital, Charlie and I went shopping. We bought the baby her first "going home" outfit, and cream puffs for the new mother. Our newest world visitor was born at exactly 3:17 P.M., on the twelfth of April. Charlie and I also picked up several trees to celebrate Morgan's birth: a blue spruce pine, symbolizing resilience; a quaking Aspen, or dancing tree, as we called it, for happiness; a Japanese maple for her beauty; and a fig tree, symbolizing abundance and wisdom.

"As I planted the trees, I prayed that this world would treat her gently while she passed through the great adventure of life. I prayed that she would be blessed with the faith, love, and courage to deal with tragedy and sorrow. I prayed that she would know the importance of integrity. I prayed that she would understand that failing is a part of life, and that there can be glory in failure and despair in success. I prayed that she would always stand up for what she thinks is right. Most of all, I prayed that our little angel would always keep in mind that she is a marvelous and powerful spirit of light.

On my way into the house, I noticed Charlie lying on a lounge chair on the patio. As she sipped water, she suddenly asked, "Mom, do you think I have angels?"

"Absolutely. According to my experience, not everyone chose to come to this world as humans. Many spirits chose not to come at all. Instead, they assist us as angels, or messengers. Do you know that translated from Greek and Arabic, that is what the word "angel" means: messenger?"

"Do you think Morgan already has an angel, Mom?"

"I think she has a few. Especially her guardian angel."

"What do you mean? How many do we get?" Charlie asked.

"There are several types of angels, each with different purposes, but they are all important."

As I turned on the water for the hose, I looked at Charlie and noticed tears rolling down her face. Quickly I ran to her. Rocking her in my arms, I asked, "What's wrong, baby?"

Sobbing, Charlie asked, "How come my angels don't help me?"

I hugged her tight, wanting to ease her pain. I said, "Angels are with us to help us carry out our plans for growth. They can help us, as long as it doesn't interfere with our free will. Sometimes it's very difficult for angels to stand by as we go through our challenges, but they know that the joy of our growth is of the utmost importance."

Charlie looked at me curiously and asked, "Are you saying that I choose this illness as part of my growth?"

Holding her by the shoulders and looking into her reddened eyes, I replied, "Charlie, I don't know your answers. You need to ask God and your angels. They are there for you. Go to your source. Ask for their assistance. Until you do that, you won't find your answers."

"Yes, I guess you are right, Mom. I will try to do that." Laying back on the lounge chair, she asked, "Do you think I can be one of Morgan's angels?"

"If you want to. You certainly have earned your wings."

Charlie laughed. "Do you really think angels have wings?"

"No," I said. "The early Christian painters seemed to have created that myth. Maybe as a metaphor for the freedom of their spirits, or perhaps they confused their light with wings."

"You mean they actually saw angels?"

"Maybe, or they remembered," I said.

Charlie looked at me and said, "What's wrong, Mom? How come you are going to cry?"

"Oh Charlie, I was just thinking how perfect God's plan is as I was planting those trees. While I played with the soil in my hands, I realized that even those who didn't make it home have a useful purpose in the universe, and they still have a chance, you know." Charlie looked puzzled. I continued. "If we could raise this world to the other dimension, we would also take them with us. It's truly a perfect and loving plan.

Charlie asked to go inside. I was leaving the patio to finish planting the trees when I heard her calling me. Quickly, I ran inside. When she saw me, she asked, "Mom, what if your mother or papá hadn't made it home? Would we have anyone to come and help us cross over? I wonder if I may have accepted to help my sisters, or someone else." She didn't seem to want an answer to her questions. I was silent. Charlie appeared to be lost in her thoughts. I sat quietly by her side. Then she asked, "Do you think I will make it home, Mom?"

I smiled and kissed her hands as I nodded yes. She smiled radiantly.

Chapter Ten

PAIN AND DENIAL

The pain in Charlie's back had started weeks ago and was getting worse day by day. The lymph nodes in her body were swelling and pressing on her spine. Now the physical pain was starting to increase. She was debating the chemotherapy issue. She had been forced to discontinue the diet after a few months, due to her inability to eat, but she just couldn't give up. She had to do something to fight.

One day she said, "Mom, I have to fight now more than ever if I want to live. I have a lot to do and I have wasted time. I have to beat this illness. Is the chemo going to be to hard on you?"

"Charlie, don't worry about me. I can take care of my feelings. I'm here for you. If you feel you want to do the chemo, go ahead, just make

sure you do it because *you* want it. Don't do it
for anybody else."

Charlie decided to begin chemotherapy now
that Ingrid's baby was born. She had waited,
thinking of how inconvenient it would be for
me to be in two places at the same time. She was
also concerned with the stress it might have
caused Ingrid during her pregnancy. The
chemotherapy was scheduled for the middle of
May. Charlie had just had a portrait taken. She
wanted to have a picture to leave for her family
if she didn't survive the treatment. Looking at
her portrait, she said sadly, "This is how I want
all of you to remember me." She sat in silence
for a long time, staring at the image of herself,
until I reminded her it was time to pick Patricia
up at the airport.

Patricia had summoned the courage to come
meet the baby and be with Charlie during the
chemotherapy. Although she was terrified and
had a hard time accepting that Charlie was
dying, especially because Charlie didn't sound or
look ill, Patricia wanted to be here for her sisters.
Charlie was ecstatic when she saw "Gordita,"

her pet name for Patricia. As they hugged, they laughed and cried at the same time.

The next morning, we went to the hospital. As we walked down the hall to the elevator, the thought crossed my mind that we were walking down "death row." Overcome by fear and help-lessness, we waited for the procedure to begin. Patricia started to feel restless, then broke down and cried. I comforted her, and once she was calmer, she said, "You know, Mom, although the word 'hospital' is derived from hospitality, there is nothing hospitable about this place. There is the feeling of total loss of control of one's life here."

"I agree," I said. "What's worse is that even if people are ill and in pain, they are expected to continually smile." Patricia got up nervously. Trying to lighten the moment, I said, "Maybe in the future we'll go to the doctor over the inter-net." Then, as an afterthought, "Gosh, maybe not. What an image, pictures of my organs pass-ing through computers all over the planet."

Patricia smiled, but seemed annoyed. "It's not funny, Mom," she said, walking back towards Charlie's room. Then suddenly, she asked, ""Did you sue the hospital for their 'faux pas,' when they overdosed Charlie during the radiation treatment?"

"No, Charlie didn't want to sue. She has worked in an emergency room. She knows that, although hospitals make mistakes by under-staffing and overworking people, it's common practice to scapegoat the staff when they are sued. Charlie feels that with lawsuits, everyone loses and nothing changes. She thinks that until laws are passed to protect the public, nothing will improve."

Taking a deep breath, Patricia said, "Gosh, Mom. If I feel so powerless, can you imagine how Charlie must be feeling?"

I explained to her that no matter how hard I tried, I could not imagine what Charlie was going through. I could guarantee her, however, that Charlie would not stay in the hospital any longer than absolutely necessary.

Two days later, I felt I had aged a hundred years, watching Charlie convulse while bottles of chemicals were pumped into her frail body. For Patricia, reality hit for the first time; she realized the seriousness of the illness. She questioned whether her sister would make it through the chemotherapy, as it was very difficult for Charlie to breathe. It was a frightening and draining experience. Finally, she was discharged. The expectation was to have the second treatment within weeks.

We prepared Charlie's room with a hospital bed, oxygen system, and everything else we thought could be needed, but she did not want her room looking like a hospital. She wanted to be at home. We quickly had to rearrange her room so that it was both cozy, and practical.

The following days were nightmarish for Patricia and me. We had to deal with the fever, vomit, diarrhea, anxiety, and hallucinations, as well as our own fears and feelings of helplessness. For Charlie it was even worse, because, in addition to the physical distress, there was mental fragmentation. She later said she felt like she had imploded and her mind had disassembled. This was terrifying for Charlie. She could deal with the physical and emotional pain and fear of her body decaying, but the thought of losing her mind was unbearable. She had hoped that during the treatment she would have a near-death experience, but instead, she many times said she had encountered the doorway to hell.

A week later, Patricia had to return to work in California. She left with a heavy heart, scared that she would never see her sister again. Days later, as she spoke to Charlie on the phone, Patricia got her hopes up because she thought she sounded so strong. Patricia convinced herself that the chemo had cured Charlie completely.

Nothing was further from reality. Charlie just seemed to get worse as the days went by. Everyday, something new added to her distress and pain. Her anxiety level had increased to the point of panic attacks. She couldn't stand to have anyone too close to her without feeling she couldn't breathe. She became irritable and startled by everyone and everything. The smell of food was unbearable. Her skin became so sensitive that just to hold her hand would make her cry in pain. Sometimes even her clothes would hurt her. Rubbing her body with lotion was no longer a relief. Taking a shower, even with a chair to sit on while bathing, would exhaust her to the point where she couldn't open her eyes.

Her hair started to fall out, completely changing her appearance. This devastated her.

Lymph nodes popped up on her neck like popcorn. She became angry with herself for undergoing the chemotherapy. For days she was moody and bitter. She constantly cried, asking, "What did I ever do that was so terrible?"

"Charlie . . . ," I tried to tell her, "I can't think of anything you could have done to bring this kind of retribution down upon yourself. I don't believe God is vengeful, or that disease of any kind is earned. This is not a punishment."

"Then why is this happening to me? I don't want to be sick. I hate it, and I will not have anymore stupid treatment. Look at me now! I was better off before. Well, if I have to die, so be it, but it will be with some dignity."

Chapter Eleven

SUICIDE

One afternoon, after coming home from work and walking into Charlie's room, I heard her say, "Mom, I can't live like this. I'm going to kill myself. I know how to do it." I was stunned. Never had I heard her talk about suicide. As a therapist, whenever any of my daughters were in crisis, I would always check with them for suicidal thoughts. Charlie had never indicated any such tendencies. I was terrified! I didn't know what to say. I left the room quickly, with the excuse of having to feed her dog Cinnamon. But instead, I went to the yard, fell on my knees, and cried in prayer. I realized that just when you think things can't get any worse, they do.

That evening we didn't talk much, but after

getting her to bed, she said, "Mom, you have to promise me that you will never tell my sisters I committed suicide."

"Charlie," I said, "I don't pretend to know how you feel, and I will not judge you. I will always love you, regardless of your choices. But I will not promise you to keep your suicide a secret. If you make that choice, you'll have to accept the consequences that come with it. You know the formula for life. You make your choices and you live with the consequences."

Angrily, she asked, "What consequences? I will be dead, remember? I won't be here!"

"You know we don't stop existing when we leave this world, Charlie."

"That's your belief, and because you say it, it doesn't make it true!"

Calmly I asked, "Charlie, didn't you say your papá was with you when they overdosed you, and how peaceful he was? As I recall, you even wanted to go with him."

"I was dreaming, or hallucinating or something," she yelled. I stood there looking at her in silence. "Are you trying to talk me out of it?"

"No, heavens no. I have learned that everyone

95

has to make their own choices. All I am saying is, you will also have to accept the consequences."

That night I cried silently into my pillow, so Charlie couldn't hear me. I struggled with my feelings, despite what I had told her. I knew from my near-death experience what the consequences would be, and I ached for her. As her mother, I didn't want her to suffer anymore, in this world or after. I wasn't walking in her shoes, however, and despite my emotional pain, I would never understand what she was experiencing. On the other hand, as a therapist, by law I have to report someone that is determined to commit suicide. But could I bring myself to report her? What would they do for her, put her in a hospital and prolong her agony? Yet, there was something so violent about suicide, my stomach ached. I didn't know what to do. I struggled with a myriad of emotions all night long. The only thing that was clear to me was that I had no objectivity. As I prayed for guidance, the name of one of my professors from the graduate school of social work, at the University of Utah, came to my mind. This brought me relief.

I decided I would go to the U of U in the morning and ask for help. I needed to get some sleep. I turned over, and my eyes caught the time. It was 5:05 A.M. Oh my, the night had gone. Suddenly I realized that Charlie hadn't even moved during the night. I felt as if I had been hit by lightning. I jumped from my bed and ran into her room. "Charlie! I called frantically. Her body was cold and completely wet. I turned on the light, frightened it was blood. I sighed with relief when I discovered that it was only perspiration. After quickly changing her bedding, then drying her, I held her in my arms to warm her up. Rocking her, I tried very hard not to cry.

She said, "I have been to hell and back tonight, and I have decided that I want to make it back home. But I sure hope I feel better."

I cried hysterically. I knew in my heart that she had transcended herself, and that she wouldn't commit suicide. It was such a relief.

Suddenly, Charlie asked, "Did you really eat

a quart of chocolate ice cream every night, when you were pregnant with me?"

I looked at her confusedly, and muttered "yeah."

She laughed. "Papá told me. Tonight, in my desperation, I prayed to God for help. I needed understanding and peace, A while later I saw a light, and in it was my papá. He sat right where you are now, and he comforted me. He told me stories of when I was born, and how I was loved. Then he held my hand and I felt a great feeling of peace. As he left, he said, 'Remember you are not alone. You are one with God.' Mom, I know my whole lifetime here on earth only amounts to maybe ten minutes in that other dimension. It's going to be bad enough to look back and think I could have done so much more. I have been letting my fear get the best of me, but that's over. I know there is life after death.

"I wanted an easy way out. I didn't even think how I would be putting you and my sisters at risk. You know, once there is a suicide, the risk of other family members or friends attempting suicide becomes higher. Even when we would like to think we are an island in the sea, we are not. The reality is that everything we do effects other people in one way or another. We all come from the same light. We are one."

That morning, as I went to work, I felt reborn. Charlie had found her source. When I walked out of the elevator at work, I ran into two psychiatrists. We talked; they asked how Charlie was doing, and how I was holding up. I murmured that I was taking it one day at a time. As I walked away, I overheard one of them say, "She's in denial." I chuckled. Little did they know the night I had lived through.

I sat at my desk, sipping a soda for breakfast. With a feeling of serenity in my heart, I thanked my Creator that we had survived one more day. I reviewed all the love I had seen thus far. I recalled the special ways that friends, acquaintances, and strangers had expressed caring and consideration for our family. Many of the Even Start families had shared the blessings of their particular faiths with Charlie, hoping for a miracle. Just about every religion had come through our home. Charlie had accepted their blessings as gifts of love. I was humbled by the thoughtful remarks and small remembrances that seemed insignificant to others, but had come to us in moments of extreme need, when we felt that to go on was impossible. I was thinking about the promises made by these spirits in their existence before they came to earth. The promises to shield, protect, care for, and assist those in need. To be there in small, seemingly insignificant ways, to buoy spirits or lend comfort. Tears bathed my face as the images of love and generosity flooded my mind. I whispered a prayer of gratitude. There was peace in my heart.

Chapter Twelve

PATIENT CURE
THYSELF

We left the doctor's office. Charlie had informed the doctor of her decision to discontinue the chemotherapy. He respected her decision and offered to help her with pain management. When we sat in the car, she said sadly, "Well, Mom, there is nothing else I can do." Then she cried. "Mom, I don't understand. How come some people can cure themselves? If this is my time to go, how come I didn't just die when I code-blued at the hospital with the Demerol overdose? Why didn't I just die there? The way everything happened, I could have gone *then* . But you were there. You seemed to intentionally stop it. You didn't allow it to happen. What was that all about?"

"So are you angry at me? I asked Charlie.

""I'm confused. I thought you had stopped me from dying because I was supposed to live longer."

"You did live longer, Charlie."

"Yes, you are right, Mom. I feel so guilty though."

"Guilty of what?" I asked.

"I read all these books that tell me I'm doing this to myself because I'm angry. That I can stop it. You know, mind over matter stuff. How come I can't make a miracle happen like some people can? How come other people can cure themselves and I can't? I don't know how. I can't make it happen and I feel so frustrated, so guilty. Why am I doing this to myself, to my family? I'm sorry. I'm so sorry, Mom, but I don't know how to make myself better. I want to live. I'm sorry," she sobbed.

Irritated, I said, "Charlie, stop it! Why are you giving away your power? No one knows what's good for you. Don't look for answers in the world. They are not out there. Charlie, take all the information that is available, then look at it and see if it fits you. If not, let it go, it's not yours. Look for confirmation inside yourself, in your heart. You are the only one that has the answers that can give you peace. Connect to your source. Nobody else can do that for you. There are many theories in the world, and they are meant to serve as guides, not absolute truths. The responsibility is ours to find the truth."

She said, "I don't know how. I don't know what to do, Mom. I'm so tired of this inner battle. I can't fight anymore."

"Maybe it's not about fighting, but about surrendering, baby. Let go, and let God," I said as I hugged her.

"I'm tired, Mom. I was so peaceful and now I'm scared again."

I held her even closer, and as I did, whispered, "When the pain becomes greater than the fear, you will find the way and understand."

"What do you mean?" Charlie asked.

"Fears have the ability to keep us prisoners. It's only when the pain, the agony, and the torture of being a prisoner become stronger than the fear, that we surrender and take the risk of trusting completely in the light of God. Remember the night you wanted to commit suicide? You found your way. Go down that same path and you will find your answers, and with them, peace again."

Chapter Thirteen

TRANSCENDING

Memorial weekend was coming up, and I suggested spending it at Snowbird, a ski resort in the mountains. I thought being together in nature would be refreshing. We could ride the tram up to the summit, where the view might offer a new perspective on things. Charlie had been unusually quiet for days, and I thought maybe a change would make her feel better. I was concerned that she was showing signs of depression. When I mentioned the idea, she got very excited and started planning. For me, being able to pretend for a moment that everything was normal felt wonderful.

At the hotel, we spent the evening watching the last episode of Star Trek, the Next Generation. Charlie even ordered food, and ate with gusto. We had a beautiful view of the mountain. She commented that the big window framed the mountain like a painting. We slept well that night for the first time in a long time, listening to the water running in the creek and smelling the fragrance of the trees as the wind caressed them.

The next morning, we awoke enthused about going up in the tram to the top of Snowbird. We carried folding chairs and pillows. The tram operator stared at us for a while, then finally said, "You can't sleep up there, you know." I wondered how he could say such a thing, looking at Charlie with her bald head and signs of exhaustion. It was so obvious now that she was dying.

Once we arrived at the top of the mountain, Charlie sat down and beheld the view. Smiling, she recalled the beautiful sunsets that she had enjoyed there. Then she said, "You know, Mom, death is definitely our most private struggle, but I'm not afraid or confused anymore. I'm at peace. Being terminally ill only forced me to acknowledge that death is real. It has been very difficult to accept. For some reason, I thought I would decide when and how I was going to die. I feel that I have grown a lot."

"How so, Charlie?" I asked.

"Well, at the beginning of my illness, I could move around and do things myself; it wasn't so hard. But as my body became less mobile, I had to learn to depend on others to help. The transition was hard to accept, but it was a learning and growing experience. The suffering, both emotional and physical, that came with this illness, expanded my ability and perceptions. Now I can understand more than I ever did before. The reason I didn't die when I overdosed was because we weren't ready. Remember how hard it was when Papá died, because it was so sudden and we felt we hadn't said good-bye? Only time helped ease that pain. If you think about it, we are fortunate that things have happened as they have, for we have been given more time for preparation. There is a whole process that needs to be completed, one of growth and acceptance. I see it now as an opportunity, a gift. This whole time, I had been talking about getting cured, and in reality it's about healing."

"Healing is what *you* call balance, Mom. Now

I think about how arrogant I must have sounded talking about beating cancer, and I feel embarrassed. I forgot that there is a higher power, and not even a leaf moves without God's will. I thought that I needed to live longer because I had greater things to do, and the whole time I was already doing them with the simplest of things."

I hugged her and said, "I believe you are right, Charlie. You have transcended to a higher state of consciousness. Do you look back now and think how foolish it was to be afraid?" Charlie laughed and nodded. "As painful as it is," I continued, "I also believe this experience may be an opportunity in disguise—a process for growth. I believe these tribulations help the people around you to grow as much as they help to refine you. You are very brave, Charlie. You have summoned the strength to accept the inevitable."

Charlie looked at me and replied, "If that is so, then you are the brave one, Mom, because, once I am gone, you will still be here, required to live. You say we chose before we came. I couldn't have made a better choice for a mother.

Your strength is something I have always admired. There was a time when I rebelled, not wanting to walk in your footsteps. I wasn't as aware, and took things for granted. But there is one thing about disease, versus accidental death. You are forced to slow down and given time to reflect. Now I have learned to see you as a human being, and less as a mother. Watching you makes me wonder if I could ever be as strong in these circumstances. I don't know how you do it. After surviving so much hardship, how do you still keep living each moment?"

"We chose each other, Charlie, and I am glad that I had the strength to be here for you during this crisis. I also want you to know, it has been an honor to be your mother. I have grown at your side, and enjoyed life with you and your sisters. I'm only one more person that your illness has touched. That is part of the plan. You know, it would have taken you at least thirty or forty years in this world to gain the insight that you have gained in this one year, and that is, if you had worked hard at it. I am so proud of you."

Charlie smiled. Then she burst out laughing

as a thought crossed her mind. "Mom, remember how tormented I was when people told me that I could cure myself? I think of that now and I smile. Bless their hearts. Their advice was well intended, but it's really people's own feelings of helplessness that they were responding to. You were right, Mom. I was giving away my power. The answers are really inside us, all we have to do is listen. This doesn't mean that I don't believe there are many truths, but only my truth is for me. I want to thank you for allowing me to find my own answers. It's like I searched everywhere, and the whole time, God was right here in my heart. If I had trusted this knowing, I wouldn't have been afraid."

Leaning her head on my shoulder, Charlie continued. "Mom, I can feel that this is my time to go, but you already know that. Right?"

"Yes," I said sadly, as I hugged her closer.

"As my life ends, there are things I wish I had done differently," Charlie reflected.

"Don't we all. The fact that you can see that now means that you have learned from your mistakes."

"Do you think I will make it back home? Is

my light strong enough that I will make it back home, to the land of my soul?"

I looked at her and replied, "Charlie, you shine in your own light." With her head on my shoulder, we hugged and sat in silence. Once again, there was peace in our hearts."

Chapter Fourteen

PREPARATION

The nights were agonizing. Every day, Charlie's body deteriorated more and more. She had resisted stronger painkillers as long as she could, with the erroneous belief that she would become addicted. But eventually gave in, due to the intensity of the pain. Upon our return from Snowbird, she started on morphine. Her right leg had swollen so much that she couldn't even turn over in bed without help. Breathing was difficult. She began picking her blankets and mumbling constantly, which were signs that the time was getting closer.

One afternoon, as I was changing her clothes, Charlie said, "Mom, there are several things I want done, once I am gone. I would like you and my sister to respect my wishes, even if you don't agree with them. Charlie had worked with terminally ill individuals before, whose final pleas were disregarded by their families. That betrayal and lack of respect seemed to be haunting her now.

"You don't have to worry, Charlie. Whatever you want will be done. I promise."

"Thanks, Mom. First of all, I want the families from the Even Start program to participate in my memorial services, just like members of this family. They've lived through these hard times with us and need to go through the grieving process too. I don't have to tell you how important they are to me. Another thing I want, is that my age not be disclosed in obituaries or elsewhere. This may seem petty, but it bothers me."

"That's an unusual request. Can I know why?" I asked curiously.

"I think we make a big deal about age. It just bothers me, that's all."

"So what am I supposed to say when people ask about that?"

"Tell them I was an adult, and I was vain." We laughed but I knew she was serious. "Now here comes the biggie, Mom. I want you to write a book about the struggle of dying, and how your near death experience helped me." Raising an eyebrow, I stared at her. "Don't give me the evil eye, Mom," Charlie said. "I know you don't like the idea because you don't think you are a writer, but I think it's important to help others through what we've experienced. You said so yourself. Only after death is no longer feared, can humanity attain a new light, and leap into a higher realm of consciousness. We are running out of time, so you need to talk, write, and lecture about it, to help others recognize and recall their uniqueness. Besides, I think you are a wonderful story teller. I remember when my friends used to come over, how you would mesmerize them, telling about your childhood. The message you have will touch people's hearts, because it's true and comes from our heart."

"Well, I can get help to do it, if that's what you want," I said.

"No," she said. "I want *you* to write it."

"Okay, I promise, but you will have to tell me what to write about. I'll do it, as long as it's understood that I am only sharing our experience, not telling anyone how they have to live. It's very important to me that people make their own choices."

"I will help you, Mom. I promise."

Later that night, I heard her talking to her father. She was saying, "Papá, your 'bebé' Ingrid has a beautiful little girl." Then she turned to me and said, "I'm telling him this as if he doesn't know."

"Does your papá talk to you, Charlie?"

"Yes, but not as we do. It's more telepathic. I can hear him in my mind. Sometimes I can hear your thoughts as well. Does that make sense?"

"Oh yes, I know exactly what you mean. That's exactly how we communicated during my near-death experience. So what does your papá tell you?"

"Papá says not to be afraid. He is here for me, and my suffering will end soon. He loves us. I'm so glad he made it home, Mom, and I'm looking forward to being with him. Now I know why, when I was taking care of the terminally ill, they would die when no one was present. The closer we come to dying, the more we need the people from the other dimension, not so much the people from this world. It's part of the preparation. Our bodies may seem pitiful as they decay with disease, but our spirits have already made the connections that we need to go home. The closer we come to dying, the greater our desire and need to reconcile with our mind, heart, and soul. Dying is definitely our most private moment, Mom."

"Charlie, I know that you promised me I would be with you when you died, but if you want to be alone when the moment comes, you are free to do so. I release you from your promise. I'll be fine."

She smiled.

I knew her time was coming and I worried about the grief of her sisters. Charlie loved Ingrid as a baby sister and Patricia as her confidant. The three of them were very close, despite the natural sibling rivalry of their youth. Each seemed to be dealing with the reality of death differently. Patricia kept her distance. She stayed away, living with the illusion that Charlie would go into remission again. Ingrid, though, spent as much time as she could with her, but asked not to be present the moment she died. I remembered how hard their father's death had been because it happened so suddenly. There had been no advance warning; the accident took all of us by surprise.

I decided that I had to do something to help Patricia and Ingrid though this ordeal. We needed to have a debriefing. The next day, I went to see one of my friends and colleagues. She was the director of a hospital grief center. When I arrived, I thought, how ironic that they would have the grief center across the street from the hospital in an inconspicuous house. Always trying to hide death and pretend it's not real.

I explained my situation, and she asked if I would consider a pre-memorial. Working with grief had made her realize how important it was to take care of things while people were still alive. I thought it only made sense to say goodbye while the dying was still here. The dilemma was how Charlie would feel about it, and how I was going to ask her.

When I arrived home, I moved around the house nervously, not knowing how to go about asking Charlie if she wanted to be present at her funeral. I sat by her and we talked about trivial things. From time to time, she would look at me and smile. Finally, she asked, "Well, when are you going to tell me?"

"Tell you what?" I wondered.

"About your conversation with your friend at the grief center."

I was surprised that she knew, because I had not mentioned my intentions to anyone, but I was not shocked. I had watched Charlie dip in and out of the other dimension. First, she would just have brief flashes of that world; later, she would stay there longer, and as she did, her awareness became universal. This is how she could read our thoughts and know our intentions.

I remember one afternoon, when I was coming home, I dozed off while driving. I almost got in an accident. I was so exhausted and shaken up, that I pulled over and cried for a while. When I got home, Charlie was lying in her bed, facing the wall. I thought she was asleep, until she said, "I'm sorry you almost got into that accident, Mom. You need to get some rest." I was startled that she knew, but got accustomed to it fast. When I mentioned it to the hospice social worker, she commented that thousands of cases have been documented where the dying know what happens before other people do. I could easily understand.

I asked Charlie, "What do you think about the idea of a pre-memorial?"

She replied, "I think it's interesting and only make sense. We don't say good-bye to people after they are gone; we do it when they are with us. Let's do it."

Immediately, she began planning. There was not much information about how to do one, so she decided it would be self-tailored. Charlie gave me a list with names of the people she wanted at the service, a small group of her friends and family. She resisted asking Patricia to come because she felt it had to be her choice.

As if Patricia had heard us, the phone rang. She said, "Mom, I don't think Charlie is going to live much longer. I will be there this Sunday."

I was surprised, but relieved. Patricia's denial had concerned me, because I thought of the guilt she would have to deal with later. It seemed, though, that she had come to terms with reality. Then I asked Charlie, "Aren't you going to say good-bye to Luis? Do you want me to call him?"

"No," she replied. "He will come and we will say good-bye."

Luis was an old friend. Charlie had known him since she was fourteen years old. Even though life took them separate ways, their friendship survived time and distance. That night Luis called. He said he'd just heard and would be arriving on Sunday. I looked at Charlie with her bald head. Her lymph nodes were swollen to the size of walnuts on her face and neck, and she had dark circles under her eyes. I asked if she wanted me to get her a wig and some make-up. She smile openly and said, "Oh, no thanks, Mom. I don't need anything like that. When I'm with Luis, I'm comfortable."

"Is there anyone else you want to say good-bye to?" I asked.

"Yes, I will tie up some loose ends with a couple of ex-boyfriends." Then, looking sweetly into my eyes, she said, "I want *you* to say good-

bye before the pre-memorial service." I agreed,
but postponed it as long as I could.

Finally, the night before Patricia arrived, I felt
the time had come. Mustering all of my
courage, I went to Charlie. She looked at me
and smiled. As I held her close, a scream, more
like a howl, tore out from the depth of my
womb. The same womb which had given her
birth was now giving her up to death. That
night I gave her permission to die. She didn't
cry. She only stroked my hair and softly
hummed a song, comforting me.

> *Ho-nay, ho-nay*
> *Sha-noon, ho-yah, sha-noon, ho-yah*
> *Hey hey yuh hey, yuk yah ho-nay*
> *Hey hey yuh hey, yuk yah ho-nay*
> *Ho-nay, ho-nay*

I looked at her and she smiled, saying, "You
know we'll be together again."

"I know," I said, "but I will miss you. Good-
byes are so painful."

"Think of the happiness on the day we meet
again," she whispered.

Later I asked her, "What was that you were
singing?" She told me it was a Native American

song that reminded her of me. It was the story of a strong willow tree that had deep, firm roots, but when the storm came, it bent so that it didn't break.

Chapter Fifteen

GOOD-BYES

I ngrid sat, looking at me for the longest time. Then she finally said, "Ma, have you gone insane? That's morbid. How am I going to go home and tell Chris that we are having Charlie's funeral before she dies? He'll think my family is weird."

"Ingrid, this is what Charlie wants, and it's how it must be. You have a choice. You can come or not. If you don't, it will be okay. If you do, bring her a farewell gift from your heart, and you can also participate. A song, poem, or anything you would like to do. Charlie has decided that the ceremony will start with a drum beat, symbolizing her heart that is stopping."

Ingrid jumped up as if stung by a bee.

"Drums? But we are not Native Americans. This is crazy!" She stomped out of the room.

Her reaction surprised me. Of all my daughters, Ingrid was the one who had a great interest and affection for Native American culture. Later, she explained that she felt it was intrusive toward Native Americans. I had said, "That's one way to look at it. You could also think of it as honoring them by including their spirituality in a ceremony that is so important to our family. Still, Ingrid was having a hard time with the pre-memorial; it sounded morbid and bazaar to her. She also felt that this was a family matter and couldn't understand why strangers were invited. "Because they are Charlie's friends," I explained, "and she wants them to come. After all, it's her pre-memorial." She left, mumbling something.

The next day, Ingrid came to my room and handed me a tape. I looked at it and started laughing. It was a Jewish song. She jumped on me and tickled me. As she laughed, she said, "Just in case. I have decided to compromise." She would come to the pre-memorial service, but she would say good-bye to Charlie in private, before the ceremony. Ingrid didn't want to share her tears with a "bunch of strangers."

Sunday morning, I picked up Luis at the airport. He appeared jovial, but in disbelief. Charlie and Luis spent the whole day talking and laughing, recapturing the joy of their friendship. I remained distant, allowing them their space. Whatever was said remained between the two of them.

Late that day, I picked up Patricia at the airport. She wanted to be strong, but as soon as I started telling her about the pre-memorial service, she cried. "She really is dying, isn't she, Mom?" I comforted her and told her that I was glad she had decided to come and spend some time with Charlie.

That night, after dinner, the whole family got together to watch some slides that Luis had brought, about his residency as a dentist in the Amazons. There was a feeling of joy. Watching them all throwing popcorn at each other and joking, reminded me of the days when the house would be full of their friends. For a moment, it felt like time hadn't passed. Yet, the reality was that an entire lifetime had come and gone.

The following day, Luis returned to Florida. He had patients to see. Charlie seemed peaceful. She later said, "We have said good-bye. That's taken care of."

I asked her if she regretted not getting married and having children. She responded, "No, I always knew I wouldn't have children. You know that. Things happen the way they had to happen. The only regret I have is of wasting time, doubting myself."

On the 4th of July, we had the pre-memorial. On a small table in one corner of the living room, we placed Charlie's portrait. Next to it were a dozen Sonia roses. Her favorite. My friend and colleague from the grief center had generously agreed to facilitate the ceremony. She beat a drum, symbolizing Charlie's heart. Charlie entered the room and lay on a mat in the center. She was dressed in her last attire, all white silk. She covered herself with a blue sheet while the rest of us sat around her. The facilitator proceeded to explain why we were there, and as the Ave Maria played one of Charlie's favorites, the facilitator burned some sage. Then, one by one, we said good-bye and gave her a gift. Some of the gifts were blessings, pictures, poems, and songs. Someone held a crystal, a symbol of both the light within, and the light towards which she was going. My contribution to the ceremony was a large pink candle, from which we all lit small white candles. The pink candle was a symbol of her love and light, and the white candles symbolized how her love and light had touched each one of our lives. Other gifts were: a picture of her deceased cat, which, in Persian culture is said to help the dying cross over; a Native American necklace, to keep away the bad spirits; a crystal heart, embodying her love/light. At the end, we had a closing song. Charlie had chosen "Somewhere over the Rainbow." The service was immensely painful for everyone involved; a tremendous amount of grief was expressed. For Patricia it was especially painful, since she hadn't been able to deal with the reality of it. The pre-memorial seemed to liberate her. Chris later commented that "It was a powerful and beautiful ceremony." After the service, the participants moved into the dining room, as Charlie had requested, to celebrate her life. Chocolate cake and strawberry ice cream, her favorite desserts, were served. The room was decorated with pink and white streamers, and the theme was unicorns.

I took the first opportunity to find out how Charlie felt about the ceremony. I thought it was helpful for everyone, but during it, I continually wondered if maybe it was too painful for her. "Charlie, was this a mistake?"

"No, Mom, it was freeing! I have never felt so free. It's the kind of freedom that comes from love. Now I can go in peace." I also could relate to the freedom that everyone expressed after the ceremony.

Later, Charlie said to me, "Here are some little gifts I want you to give Morgan, and to some of my friends."

"Do you want to give all of these to Morgan? What if I have other grandchildren?" I asked her.

"Then they won't need any of these gifts to remember me. I will know them before they come to this world."

Chapter Sixteen

HEADING HOME

After the pre-memorial service, Charlie asked that Patricia spend some time with her. It was as if they had to make up for her absence. Ingrid also spent some time, as she would come over with the baby. I felt relieved that Patricia was home, and thought that maybe I could get some rest because I felt exhausted. But at night it was hard to sleep. Charlie had a difficult time breathing. With every breath that she took, her lungs gurgled and wheezed— sounds that bellows make as they try to keep a flame alive. Many nights I lay in my bed, listening to her tired lungs struggle for air. Feeling like my heart had been ripped out, I cried and prayed that her agony, and ours, would end soon. Sometimes, as she would stop breathing to sip water, I would jump out of my bed in terror, thinking she had died. I had made her a promise. I would help her when the time came for her to take her last breath.

It was July 17th, a Sunday morning. I was in the kitchen, arranging 100 Sonia roses that the participants from the Even Start program had sent Charlie. At 12:45, Patricia called to me and asked me to help her change Charlie's shirt, as she had spilled water on herself. I went in to help her move from the recliner. The chair provided the most comfortable position and the most relief that she could experience at this time. It helped keep her swollen leg elevated, and decreased her pain.

As I lifted Charlie to move her to another chair, I realized that the response from her body was like that of a broken doll. I knew what was happening. The time had come. I felt a painful lump in my throat, but I remembered the promise I had made to Charlie, to help her in her last moment. I took a deep breath and said a silent prayer, asking for strength. Calmer, I sat down on the bed and held her bald, cold head against my chest while I kissed her good-bye.

Then I coached her to take a deep breath through her nose and exhale it through her mouth. I asked Patricia to help me lay her on the bed, and told her the time had come. Charlie started panicking because she couldn't breathe. Patricia began to cry and said that we needed to call 911, but I held her hand and begged, "No, let her go, Patty." She cried silently and nodded her head, agreeing.

Charlie was gasping for air. I coached her to breathe while I cradled her head. This calmed her. She completely lay down, and I kept coaching her to inhale through her nose and exhale out her mouth, as I caressed her face. She was breathing very slowly. She looked at us and smiled. Then, she looked over and beyond us, as if she was seeing someone above our heads. Her papá, I thought, who had agreed to be her father in this world, and now would guide her on her journey home. Charlie smiled again. At that moment, she took her last breath. I closed her eyes and said aloud, "It's over, baby. You are on your way home."

Patricia was already at the phone, calling Ingrid. "Penquenita," I heard her cry into the receiver, "she's gone." Then there was a long pause, during which I pictured Ingrid's tears. "At 12:47," Patricia finally said.

Charlie's rebirth was complete. I sat on the bed, looking at her lifeless body. I had dreaded this moment, yet, there was absolute peace in my heart. I knew I would deal with the loss, grief, and loneliness . . . later. But in that moment, there was absolute peace. I smiled, thinking that there was no more pain for her. She would now be feeling peace and love like she had never known. I mentally followed her journey home while I looked at her body, the case that had carried her spirit in this life, and now released it. I knew her destination, and in knowing, felt peace. Smiling, I closed my eyes, a little envious of her adventure.

Chapter Seventeen

PEACE

Returning to my current surroundings, my eyes focus. The fire is dimming. Suddenly, I notice that the wind outside no longer rages. Looking through the window, I see the storm has stopped. A last leaf falls from the tree. Up the street, children make angels in the snow. The silence is peaceful. It's the calm that comes after the storm.

Thanks

Gratitude is not always easy to express. However, I would like to extend my thanks to the following people for being there unconditionally for us.

Karen Adams, Sonia Aguilar, Fares Arguello, Donna Anderson, Kay Babcock, Joyce Barnes, Bob and Tricia Benes, Marian Billeter, Rhenda Bracken, Michelle Brackbill, Lonnie Bradley, Scott Bringhurst, Jodi Brown, Marnae Burdette, Lucy Chinchilla, Jamie Cohen, The Colombian Colony, Sherrianne Cotterell, Bill Cox, Barbara Cromar, D' Marie, Terina Darcey, Kent DiFiore, Heather Dunham, Julie Easton, Diane Ellington, Bill Endy, Even Start participants, Luis Fierro, Margaret Franchow, Jude Frederick, Terry Jenkins, Lynn Johnson, Miriam Guzman, Teresa Gutierrez, Susan Hayes, Elizabeth Hickey, Highland View First Ward, Karen Horman, Craig, Renon, Carri, Robb, Julie, and

Geoffrey Hulet, Steve and Susan Kaelin, Arda Klossner, Wendy Klossner, Jeannie Lee, Mimi Levine, Gladys and Wilford Lundskog, Jaime Manrique, Art and Mercedes Marshall, Keith Martin and family, Sue McPherson and family, Karen Morai, Barbara Morrell, Laura and Steve Nielsen, Darlyne and Ray Olson, Mary Ann Owens, Patty Parkinson, Richard Parks, Toni Lee Peterson, Carol Poulsen, Nano Podolski, Gloria Ramirez, Charissa Rudd, Carolyn Sanders, Kathy Sedlack, Brian and Constance See, Mary Ann Small, Dorothy Solomon, Gail Stockslager, Margaret Thorton, Jay and Barbara Thueson, Less Tippets, Joyce Toohey, Luz Alba Toro, Ursula, Rosemary Valentine, Evie Vallo, Jim Van Slooten, Helen Walters, Bob Yeates, Jay Youell, Patricia Yorksetter, Graciela Zamora and family.

Most of all, I want to thank my daughters Ingrid and Patricia, my son-in-law Christopher, and my granddaughters Morgan and Katherine.

About the Author

Frances Gomez is a licensed clinical social worker. She graduated from the University of Utah and is currently a psychotherapist in private practice.

In addition, Frances provides hospice work for terminally ill patients and their families at Vista Care. She is also a member of IANDS, the International Association for Near Death Studies. Frances currently resides in Salt Lake City, Utah.

Any responses, book orders, or poster orders can be sent to:

> Frances Gomez
> P.O. Box 520433
> Salt Lake City, UT 84152–0433

For speaking engagements, please call:

> (801) 487–6721